Personal Construct
Counselling in Action

Series Editor: Windy Dryden

SAGE's bestselling *Counselling in Action* series has gone from strength
to strength, with worldwide sales of well over 250,000 copies. Since the
first volumes in the series were published, the number of counselling
courses has grown enormously, resulting in continuing demand for
these introductory texts.

In response, and to keep pace with current developments in theory and
practice, SAGE are pleased to announce that new and expanded editions of
six of the volumes have now been published.

These short, practical books – developed especially for counsellors and
students of counselling – will continue to provide clear and explicit
guidelines for counselling practice.

New editions in the series include:

Feminist Counselling in Action, Second Edition
Jocelyn Chaplin

Gestalt Counselling in Action, Second Edition
Petrūska Clarkson

Transcultural Counselling in Action, Second Edition
Patricia d'Ardenne and Aruna Mahtani

Rational Emotive Behavioural Counselling in Action, Second Edition
Windy Dryden

Psychodynamic Counselling in Action, Second Edition
Michael Jacobs

Person-Centred Counselling in Action, Second Edition
Dave Mearns and Brian Thorne

Psychosynthesis Counselling in Action, Second Edition
Diana Whitmore

Transactional Analysis Counselling in Action, Second Edition
Ian Stewart

Standards and Ethics for Counselling in Action, Second Edition
Tim Bond

PERSONAL CONSTRUCT

COUNSELLING

Second Edition

Fay Fransella and Peggy Dalton

SAGE Publications

London • Thousand Oaks • New Delhi

First edition published as *Personal Construct Counselling in Action* 1990
Reprinted 1992, 1993, 1995, 1998
This edition first published 2000

SAGE Publications Ltd
6 Bonhill Street
London EC2A 4PU

SAGE Publications Inc
2455 Teller Road
Thousand Oaks, California 91320

SAGE Publications India Pvt Ltd
32, M-Block Market
Greater Kailash – I
New Delhi 110 048

British Library Cataloguing in Publication data

A catalogue record for this book is
available from the British Library

ISBN 0 7619 6614 5
ISBN 0 7619 6615 3 (pbk)

Library of Congress catalog record available

Typeset by M Rules
Printed in Great Britain by Biddles Ltd, Guildford, Surrey

CONTENTS

ACKNOWLEDGEMENT

We wish to thank Windy Dryden, the editor of this series, for his help during the writing of this book.

PREFACE

Personal construct counselling is as much to do with approaching a client with a particular frame of mind as with specific theoretical details about what one might do and specific techniques one might use. This book is designed to provide the reader with a clear idea of what this frame of mind is and the important theoretical ideas that underpin the counselling endeavour. No one will become a personal construct counsellor simply by reading this book, as counselling can only be learned through supervised practice. But the reader will gain some idea of how we work within that frame of mind and some of the specific theoretical concepts and techniques we use.

You may well find some of the techniques that have arisen from within personal construct psychology of use in your attempts to understand those with problems, whether or not you find the personal construct approach of value in itself. References will be provided at the end of the book for those who would like to study the psychology of personal constructs in greater depth.

THE LANGUAGE

The aim of this book is to present you with theoretical constructs without also drowning you in the associated jargon. For jargon there is in plenty.

The problem with any new theory is to present the ideas in a comprehensible way – that is, using everyday language – yet also to divorce the new ideas from the implicit, personal meanings we come to attach to those everyday words.

Kelly sometimes felt it was necessary to create new definitions. For instance, he describes 'aggressiveness' in terms of what the person *himself* is doing. It becomes 'the active elaboration of one's perceptual field'. You are aggressive whenever you go out and try something new – like reading this book about personal construct counselling. The term itself carries no value – it does not say whether or not your reading of this book is a good or a bad thing to do – that will be up to your own unique personal way of construing.

We feel that it is important not to use masculine terms all the time. Man may well include all mankind which, by definition, incorporates woman, but when reading books it does not always feel like that. Our unsatisfactory solution is to use 'him' and 'her' interchangeably and the plural 'they' and 'their' after such singular nouns as 'the client'. This is clumsy but we think it better than such unreadable solutions as 'he/she' or 's/he'.

THE PRACTITIONERS

Kelly wrote his two-volume work primarily with psychology students in mind. But personal construct psychology is being found useful by many groups of people other than psychologists. This book is therefore written for all those who are in the business of helping others. This large group includes speech, occupational, art and music therapists, the clergy, social workers, nurses, personnel managers, general medical practitioners, probation officers and trainers, as well as psychologists, psychiatrists, psychotherapists and counsellors.

At the start of his first volume, Kelly wrote a piece 'To whom it may concern'. He concludes it thus:

> To whom are we speaking? In general, we think the reader who takes us
> seriously will be an adventuresome soul who is not one bit afraid of
> thinking unorthodox thoughts about people, who dares peer out at the
> world through the eyes of strangers, who has not invested beyond his
> means in either ideas or vocabulary, and who is looking for an ad
> interim, rather than an ultimate, set of psychological insights. He may
> earn his living as a psychologist, an educator, a social worker, a

psychiatrist, a clergyman, an administrator – that is not particularly relevant. He may never have had a course in psychology, although if he has not been puzzling rather seriously over psychological problems he will most certainly be unhappy with his choice of this book. (Kelly, 1955: xi)

Once again it must be stressed that this is not a 'cook-book'. Any training in counselling takes time and effort and involves supervised practical experience. The Centre for Personal Construct Psychology in London ran a postgraduate course for counsellors and psychotherapists for many years. It was considered necessary that those accepted for the diploma course should attend part-time over a three-year period. That course is now run by Personal Construct Education and Training. Details can be obtained from Peggy Dalton.

However, not everyone wants to make such a long-term commitment. Kelly's ideas have been found useful by many who incorporate them into their existing counselling framework. It is for these people and as a whetter of appetites that this book is written.

1

The Ideas behind the Action

It is of fundamental importance to understand that personal construct theory is not a theory of counselling. It is a theory that George Kelly proposed in 1955 to explain how you and I go about the business of trying to make sense of the world in which we live. It is, in fact, not so much a theory as a total psychology of human understanding and experiencing. It is total in that it suggests we look for explanations of all behaviours, feelings, motivations, learnings, experiences and whatever else besides, *within each person.*

This approach to human understanding involves looking for explanations of someone else's behaviour by putting oneself in that person's shoes and looking at the world through that person's eyes. For instance, on occasion we may seem to lack 'motivation'. But that is usually someone else's view – we are not doing what *they* think we *should* be doing.

Most of us have a tendency to explain other people's behaviour from our own vantage point. When we call someone aggressive we do not always ask ourselves what that person thinks he or she is doing. We look at the behaviour and that is enough – we interpret it in our own terms. But for Kelly, the explanation has to be sought from within that 'aggressive' person.

Another starting point for our understanding of ourselves and others is the basic assumption that we are all constantly on the move, never stopping. If this is our starting point then we do not have to concern ourselves with what 'motivates' or 'drives' people. Each one of us is *acting upon* the world rather than *reacting to* it.

In order to be able to offer a way of looking at the totality of human experience, Kelly had to pitch his ideas at a very abstract level. This leaves us the task of filling in the content – as you will soon see. To help gain a better understanding of personal construct theory and its measuring technique, which has come to be called the *repertory grid*, we need to take a glimpse at the person who wrote the theory.

A PERSONAL HISTORY: GEORGE A. KELLY

George A. Kelly was born in 1905, published his *Psychology of Personal Constructs* in the United States of America in 1955 and died in 1967. He did not start out to be a psychologist but rather, in his young days, saw himself as an engineer. His first degree in 1926 was a Bachelor's in physics and mathematics. From there he moved on to a Master's degree in educational sociology and then to Edinburgh, Scotland, where he took a Bachelor of Education degree. In his 'Autobiography of a theory' (1969a) he talks of the four years leading up to his Doctor of Philosophy degree (on stuttering) thus:

> I taught soap-box oratory in a labor college for labor organizers, government in an Americanization institute for prospective citizens, public speaking for the American Bankers' Association, and dramatics in a junior college . . . I had taken a Master's degree with a study of workers' use of leisure time, and an advanced professional degree in education at the University of Edinburgh, and . . . I had dabbled academically in education, sociology, labor relations, biometrics, speech pathology, and cultural anthropology. (Kelly, 1969a: 48)

In the early 1930s, Kelly went to the Fort Hays State University in Kansas. Here, apart from teaching psychology to the undergraduates and doing the other things university teachers do, he became particularly involved in developing clinical training programmes for psychologists. The most remarkable feature of this period was the start of his travelling clinics. These were set up to identify the problems of school children and to make recommendations for dealing with those problems.

Kansas is a large state and a typical schedule for Kelly and his four or five students would be a 3.00 a.m. start so as to be ready to work on site at 8.00 a.m. at a school within that state. Up to twelve children would be seen each day and given a very comprehensive physical and psychological examination. While the tests were being administered by his students, Kelly would give a public lecture followed by time for questions. After lunch, until early evening they would be immersed in case conferences at which they would decide what recommendations to make about each child. These recommendations were then given to parents and teachers after dinner. Zelhart and Thomas (1983), who give us these early facts about Kelly and his travelling clinic, comment that 'a unique feature of the clinics was a 2-year follow-up by mail'.

The origins of repertory grid technique (see Chapter 4) as it exists today are rooted in this early time. By the early 1940s he had outlined 'fixed role therapy'. The development of his theory, the 'psychology of personal constructs', was under way.

George Kelly worked for the navy during the Second World War as an aviation psychologist and was involved in pilot training. Soon after the war ended he was appointed Professor and Director of Clinical Psychology at Ohio State University. During the twenty years he was to remain there he published his two-volume work.

There is a story (Maher, 1985) that he never expected any publisher to take an interest in his work. But, under some unknown internal pressure, he decided he should at least test this out, so he and his group of clinical students put twenty manuscripts of the two volumes into twenty very large boxes. (There are over twelve hundred pages in the books and the manuscript was double spaced.) These were piled into a van and delivered to twenty publishers. To George Kelly's enormous surprise, six of these publishers offered him contracts. Brendan Maher commented that he believes Kelly never really got over this error of judgement!

After the publication of his theory, Kelly was much sought after as a visiting teacher and lecturer. He travelled around the world talking about his theory and its applications. Yet the theory did not receive the immediate recognition within psychology which his personal acclaim might have led one to expect.

In 1965 he moved to Brandeis University where he died a year later leaving a book on *The Human Feeling* uncompleted. Many of the chapters drafted for this book have been gathered together in *Clinical Psychology and Personality* (Maher, 1969).

THE TWO ASPECTS OF THE PSYCHOLOGY OF PERSONAL CONSTRUCTS

The total approach can best be understood if we look at Kelly's ideas 'as if' he actually wrote two theories. One theory is to do with how we, as individual human beings, experience our world; our loves and hates, ecstasies and depressions, anxieties and guilts. The other is the theoretical skeleton pitched at a very abstract level; this provides the *framework* for our understanding of our experiencing of events.

There is a vital driving force that permeates both these aspects of Kelly's ideas – his philosophy.

The Philosophy Underlying the Theories

Kelly called his philosophy 'constructive alternativism'. This is not as incomprehensible as it may at first sound. It basically means that we have 'alternatives' with which we can try to make sense of (or construe) each other, ourselves and the world swirling around us.

Constructive alternativism underlies all of Kelly's theorising. It is very unusual for a psychological theory to have its philosophy spelled out like this. We let Kelly himself describe it:

> Like other theories, the psychology of personal constructs is the implementation of a philosophical assumption. In this case the assumption is that whatever nature may be, or howsoever the quest for truth will turn out in the end, the events we face today are subject to as great a variety of constructions as our wits will enable us to contrive. This is not to say that one construction is as good as any other, nor is it to deny that at some infinite point in time human vision will behold reality out to the utmost reaches of existence. But it does remind us that all our present perceptions are open to question and reconsideration, and it does broadly suggest that even the most obvious occurrences of everyday life might appear utterly transformed if we were inventive enough to construe them differently. (Kelly, 1986a: 1)

There are, of course, constraints. For example, we have all developed within specific social contexts and this has influenced the range of constructs we might usefully develop. The Eskimos (Inuits) may well have ten constructs to do with snow, most other people do not. We have never been confronted with enough examples of snow among which to make

4

useful discriminations. We each have a construing system that has only a finite number of ways of viewing the world.

Kelly is not saying that *any* ways of construing are possible. When he says that there are always alternative ways of looking at any event, he is talking of potential. Give us enough experience of different sorts of snow and we may well find it useful to start to elaborate our 'snow' subsystem of constructs.

Many women's groups focus precisely on this active elaboration of a construing subsystem. They attempt to make women conscious of their construing of themselves as women *in the context of a man's world*. Women are often unaware of many of the ways in which their construing limits their freedom. *And, by reconstruing, women may find alternative ways of looking at their roles.*

The essential message for the personal construct counsellor is that change is always possible for any client. But that does not mean it is easy. It just means that we can be ever hopeful that our work with the client may open up as yet unexplored avenues. 'No one needs to paint himself into a corner; no one needs to be completely hemmed in by circumstances; no one needs to be the victim of his biography' (Kelly, 1955: 15; 1991: Vol. I, 11).

We Are Personal Scientists

What sort of person is this 'him' or 'her' and how can we stop being painted into a corner? Kelly did not see eye to eye with Freudian or behavioural theorists. One of the reasons was that he felt neither did justice to the striving and personal actions of each and every one of us. Not surprisingly with his background as a physicist, he asked what new insights we might get if we were to view each one of ourselves 'as if' we were all scientists. Not pushed and pulled by events but struggling to understand our world. Just as scientists do. This was very much in accord with his philosophy which states that no one person has direct access to the truth – each looks at the world from their own, personal perspective. *There are always alternative ways of looking at events.*

We are seen as scientists in that we have mini-theories about what confronts us in the world; we conduct experiments to test out hypotheses derived from these theories; and look to see whether we are more or less right or wrong. There is nothing in here to say that we will be 'good' scientists. In fact, many of our problems are the result of our conducting 'poor' experiments – poor for us as individuals and *not* poor against some external values. Shy young Kate can never face a public occasion without a stiff whisky to give her confidence. Everyone thinks she is charming and full of self-composure. But *she* knows that is not so. She is full of whisky. Her behavioural experiment is a success to outsiders, but serves her poorly. She never puts her 'shyness' to the test. Has she learned nothing? Would she really be so shy now without whisky to support her?

This model of the person as a scientist has a very radical feature tucked inside it. Normally speaking scientists conduct experiments to study the effects of certain 'variables' on behaviour. In Kelly's model *behaviour itself becomes an experiment*. Behaviour is part of the process rather than the end product. We test out the rightness or wrongness of our own construing by putting it to the test – *by behaving*. Kate conducts the same behavioural experiment again and again, rather than the one that would allow her to move on – such as 'can I now be confident *without* whisky?'

Kelly put the inquiring nature of behaviour like this:

> Instead of being a problem of threatening proportions, requiring the utmost explanation and control to keep man out of trouble, behaviour presents itself as man's principal instrument of inquiry. Without it his questions are academic and he gets nowhere. When it is prescribed for him he runs around in dogmatic circles. But when he uses it boldly to ask questions, a flood of unexpected answers rises to tax his utmost capacity to understand. (Kelly, 1986a: 5)

In Kelly's theory *all* our behaviour is seen as testing out our construing. Most of the time we do not consciously think, 'I am now going to walk on that surface which I construe as a *floor*.' Implicitly, however, whenever we do walk on a *floor* we predict that it will be solid and immovable and will stand our weight. We also predict what it will not be: for instance, that it will not prove to be alive, nor make a loud noise. Of course, a great deal of our construing, particularly that concerning people, is much more easily invalidated and often takes place at a more conscious level. But it need not do so.

THE NATURE OF CONSTRUING

The psychology of personal constructs is a very complex and comprehensive psychological theoretical system described in very great detail. It is not our aim to submerge you in theoretical concepts for the sake of academic purity. But it is necessary to mention many of its theoretical ideas because *the process of personal construct counselling is the process of understanding the client's construing of the world as seen through the eyes of personal construct theory and, thereby, being in a position to facilitate the client's reconstruing of life and experience.*

Kelly sets out the bare bones of his theory in the form of an engineer's blueprint. It has a Fundamental Postulate which is elaborated by eleven corollaries. Like a blueprint, every word of each is defined! An outline of these can be found in the book *Inquiring Man* (Bannister and Fransella, 1986) and in *A Psychology for Living* (Dalton and Dunnett, 1992).

The essence of any theory is stated in its fundamental postulate, and we use this to provide a deeper grasp of the essentials of the approach. The postulate states that *a person's processes are psychologically channelised by the ways in which we anticipate events.* Its starting point is therefore the *person.* The theory may turn out to be useful in increasing our understanding of organisms, lower animals and societies. But they can wait. Kelly is talking about someone we think we know, or would like to know – such as you, or Peggy or Fay.

The person has *processes* that express themselves in what is often called 'personality'. Kelly's focus on process means there is no need for other notions such as dynamics, drives or motivation. Freud, for instance, had to propose the idea of 'psychic energy' to explain why we, essentially inert matter, do anything at all. Behaviourists talk of 'drives' to explain activity. Kelly's starting point is that we are dealing with the person who is *already in motion.*

The Fundamental Postulate also says that it is a *psychological* theory. This is Kelly's way of emphasising that there is no commitment to the concepts of other disciplines, such as physiology or chemistry. The philosophical position allows us to see these other disciplines as also based on human-made constructions rather than statements of reality.

The fourth term in the postulate is 'channelised'. Kelly chose this jargon word simply because it was less likely than others to imply the existence of some dynamic or underlying energy system.

The Fundamental Postulate ends with a statement specifying the nature of the 'channelising' of the person's processes – that is, our *ways of anticipating events.* This makes personal construct theory a forward-looking rather than a reactive psychology.

In practice, the Fundamental Postulate and its eleven corollaries give us a particular perspective when trying to find an answer to someone's outwardly weird behaviour. To the personal construct counsellor, that person is elaborating his ways of dealing with the world in order to increase his ability to anticipate events. That is his stance even though, at the moment, the behaviours may look self-destructive. Only by understanding the personal perspective can the counsellor glimpse the reasons for those behaviours. Only then may we be able to help the client change.

An important implication of the Fundamental Postulate is that the psychological initiative always remains a property of the person – it is we, as individuals, who do what we do, nobody else does it *to* us. Neither past nor future events in themselves can be regarded as basic determinants of the course of our actions – not even the events of childhood. It is what we make of them which forms the basis of our subsequent anticipation of events that is Kelly's basic theme for the human process of living. This does not mean that we merely gravitate towards more and more comfortable organic states. It means that confirmation and disconfirmation of our predictions are given greater psychological significance in personal construct psychology than rewards, punishments or the reduction of drives.

Reconstruing in daily life as well as in the counselling room is often rooted in disconfirmation of our anticipations. An unexpected reaction from someone may lead us to question our own behaviour rather than immediately say the other person is wrong. Invalidation or disconfirmation of our predictions can be a disturbing event. For example, many have an unquestioning belief that the crescent moon is shaped such that the man-in-the-moon can sit on its up-turned lower end and swing his legs about. Our childhood picture books have assured us that this was how it is. The implicit prediction, carried over from childhood, is that when you construe something as a *crescent moon* it will always be that way up. That prediction will be suddenly and traumatically invalidated when you first see a crescent moon in Australia. *It is upside-down!* The perception of that invalidation is not something that simply goes on in our 'thinking', it is experienced as quite sudden and disquieting 'feelings'. Thinking and feelings cannot be separated out.

GOODBYE TO DUALISM: MIND AND BODY ARE ONE

The 'body–mind' dichotomy is still a widely accepted view today. People who argue that personal construct counselling is a cognitive approach fail to grasp that Kelly wrote a theory about human experience. This means it is essentially a theory about change. Construing is not 'thinking' *or* 'feeling' – it is the act of discriminating. It is the ways in which we have perceived – at some level of awareness – that certain events around us are repeating themselves and are thereby different from other events. Once we have noted similarities and differences (discriminated) between events, we can anticipate future events. We may make the discrimination with our guts – at a non-verbal level of awareness – or make it in words. It is all construing.

Of course, our client may construe things differently from us. She may well construe *body* and *mind* as separate systems which 'interact'. It makes no sense to us as personal construct counsellors to say 'the body and mind interact' because, to us, they are not separate systems. But it is the client's construing we are trying to understand so that we can talk her language. We may therefore talk with her 'as if' we believed they were separate entities too.

As we have said before, we are forms of motion. As Kelly points out, we have to take account not only of the fact that *we* are processes, but also the fact that the events we construe are processes:

> The substance that a person construes is itself a process – just as the living person is a process. It presents itself from the beginning as an unending and undifferentiated process. Only when man attunes his ear to recurrent themes in the monotonous flow does his universe begin to make sense to him. (Kelly, 1955: 52; 1991: Vol. I, 36)

Of course, we may not always want to go the way that process seems to be going and we will sometimes resist that change. But the very act of resisting is, in itself, part of the process. We will have changed after having resisted the preceding change.

DIFFERENT LEVELS OF AWARENESS

Kelly suggests that an alternative way of looking at this body versus mind, thinking versus feeling issue is in terms of 'levels of awareness'. It is all construing. It is just that we are more consciously aware at some levels than at others. The uncomfortable feelings that accompany a behavioural experiment that goes wrong are as much construing as is verbally extolling the beauties of a red sky at twilight.

At the lowest level of awareness are those pre-verbal constructions we formed before we had the advantage of speech and still carry around

9

with us. This construing sometimes takes us unawares such as when our body tells us that we do not like the person we are shaking hands with – but we cannot immediately say why.

ALL CONSTRUCTS HAVE OPPOSITES

First, a word about the meaning of the term 'construct'. While 'construing' is the term used for describing the *process* of predicting and thereby making sense of our personal world, 'construct' is the term used for the precise basis on which that prediction is made. They are similar in that both terms involve the abstracting of similarities between items. However, the term 'construct' does differ from the notion of a 'concept' in two major senses. It involves the idea of personal action – it has prediction embedded in it – and constructs are dichotomous. Implicit in most of what has been said in this chapter is the idea that all construing and constructs are bi-polar – and constructs have two poles. It is through an organised *system* of bi-polar constructs, developed over our lifetime, that we gaze at our personal world and which gives it personal meaning.

Kelly wrote at some length on the differences between the bi-polar or dichotomous nature of his 'construct' and classical logic. He argues that both similarity and contrast are essential to the meaning we give to events. Traditionally, those events which are similar form a 'concept' and those that do not share similarities are seen as irrelevant. Personal construct theory, on the other hand, says that we cannot understand what is *good* without having some idea of what is *bad*, nor *saints* without *sinners*, nor *order* without *chaos*, nor *crescent moon on its back* without *crescent moon facing downwards*.

One of the important aspects of seeing all human construing as oppositional is that, when we predict something will be or will happen, we also predict that certain other things will *not* be or will *not* happen. We all probably expect that a tree will bear leaves and have branches and that it *will not*, for example, pick up its trunk and walk. Likewise, we may expect an elephant to have a trunk and also expect that it *will not* sprout leaves and branches and take root.

Construing goes beyond dictionary definitions. It is more than the words. Very often it is in the opposites that the truly personal meaning of construing becomes evident. At this level, construing is individual and personal. For example, two people may find it useful in giving meaning to events to use the construct *friend*. However, for one person the opposite of a friend is *an acquaintance* whereas for the other the opposite is *enemy*. It seems likely that quite different behaviours would be expected from these two people when confronted with someone placed at the opposite pole to *friend*. The bi-polarity of a person's construing is not always too clearly understandable. *Have to behave to maintain consistency* and its opposite *don't get caught out*, or *aggressive* and its opposite *nurturing*, are constructs that are probably not used by all readers. It is only by gaining insight into both poles of a construct and the relationships between constructs within the system that one can come to understand personal world views.

Taken in a global sense, the personal construct counsellor may well find it useful to ask the question 'what is my client *not* doing by doing what she *is* doing?' The possible answers are often very enlightening and contribute to a more comprehensive understanding of the client.

CONSTRUING EQUALS EXPERIENCING

Personal construct theory is a theory of experiencing. Our construing of our world *is* what we are experiencing. When we have been liberally enjoying ourselves at a party, our construing (experiencing) of that occasion will probably be different from our construing (experiencing) of an event involving sticking stamps on envelopes. Our bodies and 'we' are one. So if we alter our bodily chemistry by pouring noxious fluids into it, we can be expected to see, construe, experience things differently from when we are without those noxious fluids. Construing does not just go on in the head. We are construing, making sense of our world, at some level of awareness whether we are doing mental arithmetic, meditating or performing acrobatics. This may seem to be labouring the point, but there is a growing, erroneous belief that personal construct theory is only about what we *think*. It is, of course, also about what we *experience*.

Kelly equates learning with experience. Learning takes place as we successively reconstrue events. We learn – we successively reconstrue – we experience. Experience is more than the moment to moment awareness of our existence. We enter ever new pastures when a sequence of our psychological processes completes a *cycle of experience* (see Chapter 3 for details). This cycle starts with anticipation and ends with reconstruction. As Kelly says:

The cycle of human experience remains incomplete unless it terminates in fresh hopes never before envisioned. This, as I see it, is no less true for the puzzled scientist than for the distraught person who seeks psychotherapeutic escape from the psychological redundancies that he has allowed to encompass him, or, for that matter, for the experienced sinner who finds in repentance, not reincapsulation within a dogmatic system, but the full restoration of his initiative. (Kelly, 1977: 9)

TRANSITIONS AND CYCLES OF CHANGE

Transitions

Transition implies change. Any change, as we all know only too well, can be disquieting. While in the process of change we are in transition, and it is around this notion that personal construct theory weaves-in emotions. We experience emotion either when some important aspect of the self is validated or when we become aware of some inadequacy in our present construing of events.

For example, a 20-stone client, who, as the result of a loosening exercise, has started to explore the idea of actually *being* a person of normal weight, may see that such a change would imply an *imminent comprehensive change of her core structures*. This is the personal construct theory definition of threat. It is the sudden realisation that, if we continue along this path, we are going to become a person we do not know well enough to *be*. The importance of 'core' constructs is discussed in a number of places in what follows concerning the counselling process. Kelly chose his terms very precisely. Here he really meant 'core'. These are constructs 'by which we maintain our identity'.

Likewise, such emotions as anxiety are linked to our lack of ability to construe what is going on around us. If there is sudden movement of everything around and beneath us we may not be able to construe it immediately. This is anxiety. Could it be a brain haemorrhage? Is it an epileptic seizure? But no, it is an earthquake. Once construed, it takes on a different perspective. We can do something about it once we have made sense of it.

Other aspects of an awareness that we have problems with our construing of the world, such as hostility or guilt, are discussed in later chapters. Indeed, these transitions play a major part in our elaboration of the practice of personal construct counselling that follows.

Cycles of Change

There are two other cycles of change apart from that to do with experiencing (see Chapter 3 for details): one to do with creativity and the other, decision making.

The creativity cycle   This is a cycle that moves between 'tight' (make unvarying predictions) and 'loose' (make varying predictions) construing. For instance, you can be quite sure (tight construing means your predictions are pretty clear) that your client is doing very well and will soon no longer need your services. The client appears on the next occasion having seemingly relapsed back to the state in which you first saw her. Your predictions are suddenly proved wrong (they have been invalidated). You find few clues to help you during that session. So you make time to sit back comfortably in your chair after she has left and let your mind wander over events. You have stopped having tight predictions about your client and have loosened your construing to a point at which you really have very few predictions about her. Suddenly you remember a particular look or sign. You tighten your construing again so as to examine that event more closely – and so on. The artist may paint creatively but also has to tighten her construing in order to make judgements about the quality of the work produced. As we shall be showing, this 'tight–loose' dimension plays a major role in the personal construct counselling process.

The CPC or decision-making cycle   This cycle is linked to the details of events rather than the construing process itself. CPC stands for Circumspection, Pre-emption and Choice. I need to decide whether or not to buy a new coat. I circumspect by looking at all the issues involved: can I afford it? Is this the right time to buy a coat, between seasons? Should I go for a light-weight or a winter coat? And so on. I pre-empt by deciding that cost is the main factor. Looking at my bank balance I decide that I really cannot afford it, so I do not buy a coat.

Clients often have problems in this area. Either they do not want to make new decisions at all and so go round and round in circles circumspecting *ad nauseam*, or else they shorten the circumspection phase and act 'impulsively'.

PSYCHOLOGICAL DISORDER AND SYMPTOMS

Being a total theory of human experiencing means that there is a particular view of every idea that impinges upon the personal construct counsellor's work. This includes definitions of 'disorders' and 'symptoms'.

A Psychological Disorder

Kelly argued fiercely against the idea of seeing people with psychological problems as being 'ill'. Such a view also implies that if a person is not ill, then they do not need to be 'treated'. Kelly, and many others, believe that the use of the so-called 'medical model' of disorder hinders our attempts to understand people and so reduces our ability to help them deal with whatever it is that troubles them.

Personal construct theory defines a disorder as *any personal construction which is used repeatedly in spite of consistent invalidation.* There are therefore no medical categories to deal with, such as phobias, depressions, anxiety states, anorexia nervosas or stutterings. Instead there are aspects of the person's construing system that are not serving the person well. The client is not able to predict events to his satisfaction. Most importantly, he is not able to find any alternative way to construe those troublesome events and so behave differently in relation to them. Kelly suggests that: 'Perhaps the proper question is not *what* is a disorder but *where*, and the therapist's question is not *who* needs treatment but *what* needs treatment' (Kelly, 1955: 835; 1991: Vol. II, 196).

In practice it is useful to view the client as being psychologically 'stuck'. As a scientist, the client is unable to conduct alternative experiments and so continue to elaborate her personal construing. Her construing may have become circular so that she keeps testing the same hypotheses over and over again. She is unable to accept the implications of what she sees. She may have moved into chaos where her construing is now so vague that she cannot hold things together long enough to test anything out. The counsellor's task is to help her tighten her construing so she can get on the psychological move again.

A personal construct counsellor tries the whole time to look through the client's system of constructs to discover what is stopping the client moving on and conducting new and perhaps more effective experiments in the world. This does not mean that a counsellor never uses terms such as anorexia nervosa, stuttering or anxiety state. They are, after all, the ways in which most people communicate with each other about those who have 'problems'. Clients have also often learned these labels. It is just that a phobia is not seen as the problem in itself – but rather it is seen as a construction evolved by the medical profession to explain a certain collection of behaviours. The answer to the client's fears is sought within that client's personal construing of the events which lead the client to become overwhelmed with panic in certain situations.

The Nature of Symptoms

As with disorders, Kelly does not linger long over symptoms. They are seen simply as the meaning a person has given to otherwise chaotic experiences. It is this meaningful experience – the symptom – which the client often presents to the counsellor in the first place. The counsellor will dwell on that complaint only long enough to hear how the client puts it into the context of his life. Client and counsellor will often both move away from these immediate pains and traumas to an elaboration of the construction system within which the pains and traumas play their part.

THE PROFESSIONAL CONSTRUCTS

As well as being well versed in the theory of personal constructs and its philosophy, the personal construct counsellor has a set of constructs that describe the process of construing. Kelly called these 'professional constructs'. We have already mentioned 'tight' and 'loose' construing. There are several others.

> These professional constructs do not refer to disease entities, or to types of people or to traits. They are proposed as universal axes with respect to which it is possible to plot any person's behavior, at any time or at any place. They are also axes with respect to which it is possible to plot the changes that occur in a person's psychological processes. In themselves, they are neither good nor bad, healthy nor unhealthy, adaptive nor maladaptive. They are like the points of the compass; they are simply assumed in order to enable one to plot relative positions and chart courses of movement. (Kelly, 1955: 452–3; 1991: Vol. I, 335)

Chapter 3 discusses these professional theoretical constructs in detail.

AIMS FOR THE CLIENT

Before moving on we need to say something about the goals for the client. These are implicit in the personal construct view of psychological disorder. The person cannot find an alternative way of looking at the issue concerning him – perhaps he is repeating the same behavioural experiments over and over again. He is 'stuck'. The aim of counselling is, therefore, to help the client find acceptable alternatives (acceptable to the client and not necessarily so to the counsellor) which enable the client to get on with the business of living, of being in action, again.

SUMMARY

The personal construct counsellor starts with the assumption that no one has direct access to *the* truth. The only truth we have access to is that within each individual person – within each client and each counsellor alike. The person we have created we can re-create, although it is here that we sometimes need help. There are always alternative ways of looking at events.

Understanding lies in our ability to see events through the eyes of another – our client.

Each person looks at their world as if through a pair of goggles (our construing system) that each of us has created over the years. By construing events we are able to make predictions about the likely outcomes of our actions. Much of our construing takes place below the level of conscious awareness.

We are seen as having a problem when we are unable to find any alternative ways of dealing with our world. We are stuck. Counselling is the process whereby we may help the client become psychologically unstuck and so get on with the business of living again. There is no place for medical diagnostic categories, although there is a need to understand the language and meanings of such categories when used by others.

The way forward for the personal construct counsellor and client is by being able to design new behavioural experiments that the client will find useful in untying the knot of their own construing – for all behaviour is seen as an experiment conducted to test out our current interpretations of the world.

We now move on to the counselling setting. This means looking at the skills and experience the personal construct counsellor needs to have when meeting the client for the first time.

2

Setting the Scene

The Counsellor in Relation to the Personal Construct Approach

The personal construct counsellor meets the client for the first time armed primarily with a particular *way* of thinking. For instance, the person is a scientist who can always reconstrue and thereby approach the world in a different way; and behaviour is an experiment rather than an end product. Reconstruing is not easy, but it is potentially possible as the philosophy says.

The frame of mind is nothing more nor less than the theory of personal constructs, its underlying philosophy and its model of the person as a scientist.

There are two important implications for counsellors embedded within personal construct theory and its philosophy. These are to do with the reflexive nature of the theory and responsibility to the client.

Reflexivity

Reflexivity is to do with turning a theory about others back on to ourselves or the theory writer. It means that the counsellor is seen as operating as much within the terms of the theory as are the clients. As the client changes his or her ways of construing events, so too must the counsellor. The counsellor has to be involved in a constantly reflexive process, seeking to make his or her own construing explicit to the self rather than leaving it implicit and thus potentially maladaptive or damaging. This makes personal construct supervision for the counsellor, in essence, also personal counselling. Fransella (1995) demonstrated the reflexive nature of personal construct theory by applying it to Kelly himself.

Responsibility

Kelly felt strongly about the responsibilities counsellors must accept whenever they embark on an initial consultation with a client. He says:

> Our general rule for listening to people confide intimate matters is that we should do so only to the extent that we are willing to accept responsibility for seeing that the venture works out well for the person who confides . . . this responsibility goes far beyond mere acceptance, for acceptance, followed by abandonment of the relationship or by simple indulgence, may do more harm than good.
>
> Listening involves a commitment. What the clinician should always bear in mind is that, regardless of whether he is accepting or rejecting, active or noncommittal, perceptive or obtuse, he creates a professional obligation for himself whenever he lets a person confide in him. (Kelly, 1955: 955; 1991: Vol. II, 277)

THE RELATIONSHIP BETWEEN CLIENT AND COUNSELLOR

As with everything else in personal construct psychology, the counselling relationship and the whole counselling setting are couched in the language of science. Counselling is a 'scientific' activity and the counselling room a 'laboratory'. 'For me the most exciting experimental situation is the [counselling] room, and the most stimulating colleague in the research enterprise is my client' (Kelly, 1969d: 155).

The relationship between client and counsellor is fundamentally based on the personal construct notion of role. A role relationship exists whenever one person attempts to construe the construction processes of the other.

As the client is seen as having had a hand in creating the problem he now presents, there is the expectation that he can re-create himself. We therefore approach the client with hope. The client is not a prisoner of his biography – although he may have made himself a prisoner by the ways in which *he construes that biography*. We do not start by looking for clues to the client's present problem in his experiences of the past; we listen to how the client construes himself in the here and now.

Since no one person has direct access to '*the* truth', the 'truth' we are interested in is that of the client. The counselling relationship is therefore essentially one of equals struggling with the same problem. The counsellor possesses no answers: the client has those. The counsellor strives to help the client come to grips with some of those answers and make one or more of them a living, workable reality.

So when we see the client for this first meeting we are equipped only with our personal construct theoretical and philosophical model, together with some skills.

SOME OF THE PERSONAL CONSTRUCT COUNSELLOR'S SKILLS

As you will see, the skills Kelly emphasises stem directly from his theory and philosophy.

The Ability to Work in the 'As If' mode

The counsellor must be happy with the 'as if' way of working. This comes from the philosophy of constructive alternativism. The counsellor acts as if her view of this client were true. Then she can see if what she expects to happen actually does happen. If it does not happen, the whole world will not collapse. She has got it wrong and must try to do better next time for the client's sake as well as her own. As counsellors, we do the very best we can in the clear knowledge that we have not cornered the market in the truth.

The 'as if' philosophy is not for the counsellor alone; the client will be asked to join in. One result of this is to allow for a variation in mood within the sessions. At some point, the client will be asked to explore her construing and to 'try on' alternative ways of looking at things. The client will learn that the laboratory of the counselling room is a safe place in which to experiment.

Subsuming

Above all else a personal construct counsellor must be able to 'subsume' a client's construing system. As we have said before, this means being able to put oneself in the client's shoes and see the world through the client's eyes.

However, subsuming is more than seeing the other person's point of view and having some experience of what the client is experiencing: it is more than empathy. You actually strive to move along those inner pathways of the other's experience for short periods of time. You struggle to put yourself in the client's shoes and look at the world as the client is doing. Simply living the other's experience for however short a time does not help because you will be as stuck with the problem as the client is. The counsellor therefore subsumes the client's construing within the system of professional constructs rather than her own idiosyncratic value-laden ones.

Suspension

The counsellor has to develop the skill of suspending his or her own construing of events so as to subsume the client's reality. The counsellor's values are of no relevance here – in fact, they are counter-productive. One cannot listen fully to another while filtering everything that is said through one's own personal values.

This ability to suspend one's own construing of events so as to subsume a client's construing system is, for the majority of people, the most difficult of all the personal construct skills to acquire.

Credulous Listening

If the ability to suspend one's own and subsume another's construing system are the vital skills a personal construct counsellor must possess, then the ability to listen credulously is the first stage of 'getting into' the client's system.

The counsellor starts listening with the belief that whatever the client is communicating is 'true'. Kelly is not advocating continued acceptance of the client's views and feelings. Credulous listening is merely the starting point. The recognition that, for the present, the client's world view is all that is important. It is valid and true for the client just as the counsellor's world view is valid and true for him. In addition to providing the counsellor with invaluable insights into the client's experiences of the world, it shows respect for the client.

As we have said, to practise credulous listening the counsellor must, literally, put her own construing system 'out of mind'. She must impose no interpretations, no values, no personal recollections upon what the client is conveying. But to suspend one's construing system without having something to take its place would be a chaotically anxiety-provoking thing to do. In place of her own personal construing system to do with the world, the counsellor brings to the fore the system of professional constructs within which she seeks to 'subsume' the construing of the client.

Observation

The skill of observation depends on the counsellor having a well elaborated personal construing system (so as to make sense of what is observed). It is also important that the counsellor has a range of experiences with people having a variety of problems. For instance, she needs to be alert for signs that the client's confusion may have neurological rather than a purely psychological basis. This is not to say that the personal construct counsellor sets himself up as a medical diagnostician – far from it. But it does mean that the counsellor must know when to seek medical or alternative advice. In many cases this could be the counsellor's supervisor.

Creativity

Every client faces the counsellor with something new. The counsellor therefore has to be creative so as to devise new techniques and formulate new constructs to aid reconstruction. This is more than using 'as if' construing. It means, as Kelly says, 'a readiness to try out one's unverbalized hunches'. He is referring here to our ability to act independently of words which has nothing to do with a person's verbal skill. In essence:

> Creation is therefore an act of daring, an act of daring through which the creator abandons those literal defenses behind which he might hide if his act is questioned or its results proven invalid. The psychotherapist who dares not try anything he cannot verbally defend is likely to be sterile in a psychotherapeutic relationship. (Kelly, 1955: 601; 1991: Vol. II, 32)

This form of creativity in counselling is closely linked with an ability to 'be active in formulating testable hypotheses and in trying them out to see what happens'. If the counsellor insists on near certainty before he is willing to explore something new with the client, neither will move far. This obviously does not mean trying out hunches impulsively. The counsellor must have thought long and hard about what it is he is asking the client to do – *in the client's own terms*. What may look at first sight to be a minute experiment from the counsellor's angle could, on examination, turn out to have massive implications for the client. But, having thought it through, the counsellor must then have the nerve to suggest that the client put it to the test.

THE CLIENT'S EXPECTATIONS OF COUNSELLING

So much for the knowledge and skills a counsellor has to sustain him or her during this first meeting with the client. But what does the client expect? As any experienced counsellor knows, there are a number of expectations a client may arrive with. These need to be discovered if the counsellor is to establish a good working relationship. Of course, it is not necessary for the counsellor to share the client's construction of counselling. But it is important to know what these expectations are in order to be able to subsume them and so decide whether or not she thinks she will be able to help this client.

It's About the Problem

This client will not want the counsellor to deviate from the 'treatment' of the 'symptom'. He may well be working within the medical model which says that, if you have a symptom, you go and get yourself treated for it. This client will not be happy if the counsellor starts too early on talking about dreams.

Everybody's Doing It

Some see counselling as an end in itself. As Kelly has said: if you have a problem you go and lie down to be treated for it rather than seeing it as something you try to solve yourself.

Counselling Makes You Better

This is a view held mainly by those who do not have incapacitating problems, but are focusing more on self-development, perhaps as 'self-actualisation'.

Counselling Under Ether

Some clients come wanting to be relieved of their problems by some form of magic – that is, without their having to do anything themselves. Quite often what they are really looking for is something like hypnosis. The discovery that counselling can be both painful and exceedingly hard work may lead them to give up before any improvement has been felt. If you think that you are unlikely to disabuse this client of the expectation of some magic, it may well be best to refer him for hypnosis with the proviso that you will be glad to see him again should he so wish. At no point should the client be made to feel rejected.

Looking for Support for the Problem

Sometimes this takes the form of providing proof that they are 'sick' and therefore cannot be expected to live a normal life. Sometimes it can be used as a punishment of parents or spouses. 'Look what a mess you have made of me, I have to have treatment.' This can be particularly punishing when the parents or spouse is/are paying for the counselling.

Seeking Counselling Itself Initiates Change

For some clients the decision to seek psychological help with a problem has far-reaching implications. These clients may seem to change very rapidly, but it will not be as a *result of* counselling, but rather that the change was all designed and ready to happen, and the counselling provided the context in which it could occur.

Clarification of Problems

Some clients take a seemingly sophisticated view of counselling; that it is something that can help sort out specific problems. This does not necessarily mean that these problems are straightforward or easy to deal with, but just that clarification is all the client needs. If, on the other hand, the client insists on seeing the problem as more to do with others' behaviour than their own, counselling is not likely to get far unless the client can come to 'own' the problem.

The Ultimate State of Passivity

Some clients seem to decide to come for counselling as a last resort. They see it as destructive of their personal integrity and therefore cast themselves in the role of helpless patient. They are literally being 'patient'. Their posture is one of helplessness and despair.

None of these expectations on the part of the client presents the counsellor with special problems – none is 'good' or 'bad'. A client is no more and no less than what she is. As in all aspects of personal construct counselling, the counsellor's job is to subsume (get inside) the client's construing system to spot ways in which the client may be able to get himself on the move again. The answers to the questions 'why have you come to see me?' and 'how do you think I might be able to help you?' will aid in this understanding process.

THE SETTING

The appointed day has arrived. You are in the frame of mind that is open to all this new client will present to you. But you know nothing of her construing as yet. You have had no opportunity to take a glimpse inside her world. What will the client make of you? What role will the client expect you to play?

There is little you can do specifically to prepare yourself for this first session with the client except get into the frame of mind that makes it possible to listen *credulously* to what the client has to say. There may, however, be two questions that will lurk in the counsellor's mind during the first session. Does the client want my help? Is my training and experience sufficient for me to help this client with his problem or will I be out of my depth? These are reasonable questions and should be made explicit.

If you are in a setting in which traditional uniform is the norm – perhaps a white coat – then your role is dictated from the start. There is something official about it. You are definitely different from the client who does not have the status symbol of the white coat. You might consider wearing clothes that do not state quite so clearly what your role is. The client can then construe the clothes – and thereby you – in a number of alternative ways.

Another point you may wish to take into account is how you present this first session to your client. One approach that is sometimes found useful is to make it clear that this first session is a one-off session. That is, it is exploratory for both parties. The client may not like you; may not like your approach; you may feel out of your depth with her; she may be wanting a type of therapy which you cannot or will not offer her. If it is seen as the first in a counselling series and, for some reason, you decide you are not the right person for her, she may feel rejected. It will certainly not help her with her problems and you would want to avoid that.

The words of Chris Thorman (1983) may help you get a 'feel' of what the personal construct counsellor and the language in which Kelly couches his psychology are about.

> If you can listen deeply, when she's expressing
>> suspending for a time your own self's view
> If you will enter his ways of seeing
>> live for a while with her anticipating
> If you can enter, but not get lost
>> subsume, yet not belittle
>>>> You might hear someone

> If you can keep your info gathering
>> whilst all around you are cramming theirs in neat nosologies
> If you can keep your propositions open
>> whilst all around you are constellating theirs
>> and pushing them on you
> If you can take positions for the use of
>> when all around you are collecting fragments of absolute 'truth'
>> and setting them in stone

> If you'll consider the implications
>> respecting his need to hold together
> If you'll look where there's room to grow
>> but give with awareness your validation
> If you can formulate a diagnosis
>> to act as a frame for your inquiring
>> but not as a cell to lock you both out
> If you can see where *you're* coming from
>>>> You might glimpse someone

> If you can watch for themes and learn her language
>> watch for threat and with her weave a freer web,
> If you can watch for times to tighten, when to loosen
>> times to push and times to ride
> If you can watch for 'affects' to changes
>> threats to core
>> anxieties chaos
>> guilts displacement
>> hostility from the status quo

If you can hear about his past without construing fossils
    to his future hopes and relate them to his present
If you can see that what suits one might break another
                    You might reach someone

If you can paint with words but not make words your master
    beyond those verbal handles go
If you can go beyond the 'common' sense
    and watch for symbols uniquely all her own
If you can catch her meanings expressed in many forms
                    You might touch someone

If you can watch for movement and move with him
    plan ahead, prepare a way
If you can take account of where she sees her problems lie
    know about her world in which she hopes to change
                    You might help someone

If you can help him reconstrue his tangled construct web
    work with, in exploration
If you can seek for windows where none appear to be
    create new paths with fruitful implications
                    You might help relieve someone

If you can help her reconstrue
                    You might help free someone.

Meeting the Client for the First Time

Just as there are no hard and fast procedures to be carried out whenever one meets a client for the first time, so the personal construct approach is not limited to the one-to-one situation meeting in private, although this is the most common setting for counselling. We will start off by giving an account of meeting a client for the first time in the usual one-to-one private setting, and then give other examples of how the personal construct principles can be applied to counselling relationships in other settings. The 'I' in the following is, of course, the counsellor.

Trixibell

Trixibell is on time. I (Fay) have been idly wondering why her parents gave her this unusual name and what other children had made of it at school – and indeed what she has made of it.

Trixibell is 35 years old, smartly dressed as befits a career woman who has some success in the banking business. Her hair is brushed softly so as to frame her face. She is taller than I am – about 5 feet 10 inches – and talks in a lively, bright, high-pitched way.

We arrange ourselves comfortably in our chairs. Since I want her to feel free to look away from me with ease I prefer the chairs not to be facing each other – I find about 90° quite comfortable. And as I will want to be sure I catch as many of her changes of expression as possible, I like to have her chair facing more towards the window or the light than mine does.

When we shook hands, Trixibell's had been moist so I start out with the idea that she is under some stress and may be experiencing some anxiety at this meeting. Most people do, so that is not a very profound observation in itself, but from a personal construct perspective it has specific meaning. She may be finding it difficult to make much sense of the situation, and may be at a loss when it comes to predicting what will happen. She can make no predictions and so has no guidelines for behaving. Such is Kelly's definition of *anxiety*. Stress is a more complex idea and is bound up with the notion of *threat*. We are threatened when we are aware that, if our interpretations of a situation are correct, we will be facing comprehensive change in some important aspects of how we construe ourselves. Stress is the awareness that threat is possible. A not unlikely prediction if Trixibell thinks the counselling may 'work'.

So I behave towards her 'as if' my hypothesis were correct; that is, that Trixibell is, to some extent at least, at a loss to know how to behave in relation to me and the situation generally. And that she has some feeling that the counselling she may decide to undergo will enable her to change. That may be what she would like to happen, but change can be an awesome prospect nonetheless.

I therefore do my best to give the occasion some structure. I take out a pencil and some paper and ask some routine questions such as her address, telephone number, marital status and so forth. This is by no means my standard practice but is done in my response to how I perceive the needs of this client. *I have begun to play a role in relation to her.* I am relating my communication with Trixibell to my understanding of how *she* is interpreting (construing) our interaction.

My strategy seems to be working. Her voice has dropped considerably although she is still talking and filling all intervals. I listen hard and I listen *credulously*. In these first minutes or even sessions, my approach to the client is one of total belief and acceptance of everything she wants to tell me. It goes without saying that a client communicates with both words and actions and what the client 'tells' is a combination of both. I am in the process of collecting impressions in these early stages and any obvious inconsistency or untruth is just as much *data* about the client as all else.

In order to listen credulously, I have to be able to put my own feelings, value systems, ideas to one side. They are 'suspended' for the duration of the session. If they intrude into my listening then they will come between me and my client. My only interest is in trying to follow (and so 'sub-sume') the pathways the client currently uses to make sense of the world. This perspective enables the counsellor to be ever diligent, ever alert for times when their own construing of what the client is experiencing threatens to distort the client's experience.

I accept my responsibility and obligation to Trixibell as I listen to her talk about her mother who 'is a pain in the neck', a 'martyr who is engulfed by self-pity'. I am not in the least concerned with whether or not her mother is actually a pain in the neck and a martyr, only in the fact that this is how she is seen by her daughter.

Trixibell describes her problem as failing to make long and lasting relationships with men. At one time she was so desperate that she took an overdose but was found and taken to hospital in time. She gives her suitors her genuine love and does her utmost to ensure the man of her choice responds likewise, but the relationship always founders. She cannot understand why.

Time is passing and our session (50 to 55 minutes) has only another ten minutes or so to run. I have an uncomfortable feeling that I have been listening to a lot of words but that I really have a very cloudy picture about the world in which Trixibell lives. I stop her, as gently as I am able, during a long description of a married woman friend with whom she has a really good relationship. I ask her 'what's going on *now*, inside you?' There is quite a long pause before she answers 'I am thinking about my friend as I tell you about her and about how lucky she is to be happily married and to have two lovely children.'

This is not what I meant. She has given me thoughts and I was after feelings. 'Yes, and can you tell me what you are *feeling* – now – this very instant.' The pause is even longer. Her face falls, her eyes mist over, tears well up and flow slowly down her cheeks. 'I am feeling how deeply I love

David – my friend's son – I have so much love to give and no one seems to want it.' A thought crosses my mind that this sounds rather as if she is saying the fault lies with others rather than herself. I do nothing with this thought – it just lies there until such time when it can be checked out.

At an initial session such as this I make it a rule never to press for or explore issues which may well be very complex and require more time than we now have available and also far more knowledge of the client than I have at present. Knowledge about the client (data) is very necessary before painful issues can be investigated. The counsellor must be aware of the potential dangers involved in such explorations. What threats and anxieties is the client possibly being asked to face?

My question has provided the data I was looking for – I now have a sudden and clear glimpse of an aspect of Trixibell's world that was causing her a problem. Whether it was *the* problem is not important at this time.

Our time together is coming to an end, and I need to be sure that Trixibell has 'tightened' her system for construing the everyday world sufficiently for her to be able to deal with it efficiently when she leaves. Having found out that Trixibell can cope well with the world at an intellectual, factual level, I ask her to give me a picture of David, what he likes, where he is at school and so forth. We talk amicably like this for a few minutes. Her tears disappear almost immediately and she appears lively and smiling again.

I now ask her whether there is anything she would like to ask me. She is interested to know about the personal construct approach. I talk along the lines that we are interested in the person's view of the world in the here and now; that we are only interested in the past if it appears important to the client – there is nothing inherently important in early childhood that means it should be explored with all clients; that we do not have any answers – the client has the answers, but we do have some skills that enable us to help the client seek answers from within their own construing of the world. I stress that we consider there to be no absolute truths since we all have our own unique ways of looking at the world; that this means we can all change our ways of dealing with the world, although it is by no means always easy; that we expect our clients to do a lot of work, including work between sessions.

I also often make a point of stressing our view that most of the 'work' is carried out by the client between counselling sessions rather than at the sessions themselves. Since all behaviour is viewed as an experiment the chances for experimentation are much greater between than within the sessions. The sessions are where the experiments are designed. If a client decides that the approach offers something they feel they may be able to use, I like to make a contract with the client about a number of sessions to which we will both be committed.

The ways in which all these ideas are worded depend greatly on the client, but the message is the same.

Trixibell decides she would like to explore her problem from the personal construct perspective and we arrange to meet for ten sessions in the first instance. I do not consider this will be enough as I have already formed an initial opinion (hypothesis) that she is going to have to undertake some fairly radical reconstruing of her views of herself – mostly involving her relationship with her mother – much of which is probably pre-verbal (developed during childhood without words attached to the constructs). Our first task may be to persuade her that some of the problem may lie in the way she behaves to others as well as how they behave to her. But we shall see.

We plan to meet next week. During the coming week, Trixibell is asked to write a 'Self-characterisation'. This is a portrait of the client written by her in the third person. There are virtually no rules about its length, content and so forth. Details of this are given in Chapter 4.

Trixibell now leaves. She appears much more relaxed than when she came and the pressure behind her talking has disappeared. We both indicate that we are looking forward to meeting again in the coming week.

OTHER SETTINGS

As we have said, by no means all personal construct counselling takes place in this one-to-one individual setting, although this is its focus in this book. The skills of credulous listening and subsuming the construing system of another along with some knowledge of the essentials of personal construct theory can be of value in many situations: that is, wherever the world of the client needs to be explored in order to relate to that person in a helpful way. A few examples of other settings follow.

A Nursing Situation

Patients in hospital are often talked of as 'regressing'. That is, they are seen as behaving in a childlike, dependent way. This behaviour is construed by many as undesirable and something 'to be dealt with'. A nurse with a personal construct frame of mind would approach a 'childish' male patient in quite a different way. Since, for her, all behaviour is an experiment, she will be asking herself what it is that the patient thinks he is doing by behaving in this way. What experiment is he conducting?

Mr Norman is a businessman who has a well organised way of construing his world of work; he is also a father and has a construing system that serves him well in that role. Suddenly he finds himself in a situation in which his main ways of construing the world just do not work. He is flooded with anxiety because not only can he not predict events around him very well, he also cannot predict himself. This anxiety is untenable.

He thrashes around and comes across a subsystem for construing events which he has not found of use for some considerable time. There was that world in which women looked after him and saw to his needs. He looks at the world through these personal construct spectacles again. They do not fit the world very well, but at least they serve him better than the chaos in the world he has been experiencing. He starts to behave in a childish way.

A nurse who has listened and heard this message will be in a better position to help Mr Norman give more structure to his illness and the general sickness role he is having to adopt. She may be able to help him place some meaning on his new experiences and so be able to construe from an adult rather than a child perspective. For a wider view of personal construct counselling for those who are physically ill the reader is referred to Viney, 1989.

An Occupational Therapy Setting

There is Winnie. She has been in a psychiatric hospital for 32 years – ever since she was 17 years old. She is a very delightful person, much favoured by the staff. She always does as she is told. She is always smiling and loves being cuddled. There are occasions when she lashes out, but these are rare. But Winnie never talks. The only way to understand Winnie's construing is to observe her. It is easy to see that her behavioural experiments nearly always provide her with the results she is seeking. No wonder she is content. She finds no need to talk to people or ask for things – they talk to her and give her things.

For some time now, the personal construct occupational therapist has been trying to construe Winnie's construing by watching her behaving. One day, as she is taking a group of patients through the hospital on their way to the pottery room, she sees Winnie slow up. The usual rather empty smile leaves her face to be replaced by a look not seen before. It is almost as if Winnie had seen something that conjured up a way of construing her world from the past – before she became this childlike Winnie. She was looking at a piano.

The occupational therapist went to the ward to look at Winnie's case notes later in the day. There, among the yellowing pages at the beginning of the massive wodge of notes, was the statement: 'It is reported that Winnie liked to play the piano.'

The next day Winnie is taken to the piano. She sits on the stool with a look of serious concentration. She starts to play. Her fingers do not do all that she seems to want them to do, but a look of deep contentment spreads over her face; an adult look which the occupational therapist has never seen before. Winnie is playing a Chopin Nocturne. In a sense, the occupational therapist feels she has met Winnie for the first time. She decides that this is the medium she is going to use in her attempts to delve into the mysteries of Winnie's construing of the world.

An Art Therapy Context

Martin is another person who does not talk. But Martin does not look happy. He is difficult with the staff, often having outbursts of violent behaviour. He appears to have given up talking when he was 16 years old. He is now 22. He was sent for art therapy because it was thought he might express something of his problem through painting. But Martin was not going to co-operate with that scheme. He just sat; day after day; staring into space.

There is never too much time to give to individual patients at the art class because many are very active and demanding. However, the personal construct art therapist made it his job to spend ten minutes each session sitting close to Martin. The art therapist would talk to Martin about anything that came into his head.

One day, as the art therapist was doodling on a piece of paper at Martin's side, he became aware that Martin's blank gaze had changed to one of focused attention. His gaze was on the doodle. It was a sailing ship. The art therapist handed Martin the pencil and turned the paper towards him. Martin took the pencil and drew a cliff with a figure standing on the edge of it. The art therapist took the pencil back and drew a figure on the sailing boat with a hand stretched out to the figure on the cliff. There was a long pause. The art therapist metaphorically bit his nails – would Martin accept the gesture; show himself as jumping off the cliff; or just cease to play the game? Martin slowly took up the pencil, heaved an enormous sigh and drew a series of curved lines. Was this a bridge? Was it a rainbow? It did not matter at this first communication between Martin and the art therapist. Martin looked the art therapist directly in the eyes for the first time. 'Nice,' he said. Martin and the art therapist had met.

Summary

The counsellor is armed with a sound knowledge of the nature of personal construct theory and its philosophy of constructive alternativism. She uses this to provide a framework within which she can understand how her client is construing his world, which in turn leads him to have the problem he presents. Apart from these and other skills, the counsellor needs to be aware of the ways in which her client may be viewing the counselling relationship and what may be required of him.

The examples have been chosen to show how the counsellor works at all levels of awareness – the highly verbal, the almost completely non-verbal, and accessing the pre-verbal through both verbal and non-verbal channels. As with all approaches, some brief descriptions of working with a client seem very similar to what might be done from the perspective of another approach. The counsellor is creative and has at her disposal any method of interacting with the client that she thinks may help that client along the path of reconstruing life.

The next chapter deals with the stage of counselling during which the counsellor actively attempts to subsume the client's construing within these professional constructs and thereby formulate hypotheses about why the client has a problem. This diagnostic stage is viewed as the planning stage of counselling.

THE FRAMEWORK FOR UNDERSTANDING PROBLEMS AND POSSIBILITIES

We are now ready to focus the sessions on collecting the data from which we will make a first attempt at formulating the nature of the client's problem. We must collect enough information to enable us to map our way forward with the client.

THE MEANING OF 'DIAGNOSIS'

Kelly felt strongly that it was not in the client's interest to have a 'medical' diagnosis made of the problem. That inevitably leads to the client being placed in a category box with a label such as 'depression', 'personality disorder' or 'anxiety state'. Kelly puts his view like this:

> The clinician, especially the psychological clinician, can rarely reduce the problem of his client to a single issue. He must see his client . . . in terms of a considerable number of dimensions. This is not easy to do. Some clinicians do not even try; they attempt, instead, to reduce the problem to one single 'diagnosis' or 'disease entity'. Having thus construed the problem preemptively, they start doing to the client all of the things their book says should be done in this particular kind of case. When a client meets this kind of clinician, he should be very careful what kind of 'diagnosis' he lays himself open to. (Kelly, 1955: 193; 1991: Vol. I, 134)

So there are no medical categories for the personal construct counsellor to use and it is therefore perhaps confusing for us to use the term 'diagnosis' at all. But there is nothing wrong with the concept itself; it is what it has come to mean that creates the problem.

The counsellor, like all counsellors, wants to help the client. To meet this aim, she must attempt to understand the present realities of the client's life (that is, how the client sees it). A further, and vital, aim follows on from the philosophy of constructive alternativism and the psychological assumptions stemming from the Fundamental Postulate and its eleven corollaries. The counsellor must find avenues in the client's construing of the world along which he and the client may move towards a solution of the client's problems. This all leads to our construing any diagnosis as *the planning stage for client reconstruction*. Kelly calls this 'transitive diagnosis' and gives it this explanation:

> So that it may be kept clearly in mind just how we approach diagnosis, we are using the term *transitive diagnosis*. The term suggests that we are concerned with transitions in the client's life, that we are looking for bridges between the client's present and his future. Moreover, we expect to take an active part in helping the client select or build the bridges to be used and in helping him cross them safely. The client does not ordinarily sit cooped up in a nosological pigeonhole; he proceeds along his way. (Kelly, 1955: 775; 1991: Vol. II, 153)

PROFESSIONAL CONSTRUCTS

In order to formulate any diagnosis you need to have some 'professional constructs' at your disposal. Kelly considered that one of the many great contributions of psychoanalytic thinking was its development of a set of constructs to do with what was going on inside the client. Like Kelly, Freud and his followers had rejected the still current procedure of making people fit certain clearly defined categories such as 'depression' or 'anxiety state'. Instead, he developed his own system of professional constructs with which to gain an understanding of the client and his problems. These included the well known complexes, repressions and mechanisms for defending the ego, such as sublimation.

The important point is that both Kelly and Freud developed a set of professional constructs as an alternative to medical diagnostic categories. Kelly's system of professional constructs indicates the more important ways in which people can change; they are *not* intended to enable one person to be compared with others: 'They are avenues of movement as seen by the therapist (counsellor) just as the client's personal constructs are potential avenues of movement as seen by the client' (Kelly, 1955: 775; 1991: Vol. II, 153)

There are two levels at which the counsellor tries to understand her client. The first is the now familiar 'seeing the world through the client's eyes' and suspending her own value system. The second involves trying to understand the client's construing through the system of professional constructs. In this second way it is possible to become partners with the client so that a plan can be designed to facilitate her psychological progress which she has not been able to make alone. The professional constructs for designing the way forward are detailed and clear.

Construing at Various Levels of Awareness

Pre-verbal and core construing   As outlined in the previous chapter, Kelly's theoretical system and philosophical approach to the person are fundamentally different from Freud's in many respects, not least in how 'unconscious' feelings and ideas are dealt with.

In spite of all her verbal sophistication, Trixibell had some feelings about herself and her need for love which she was quite unable to put into words. This, combined with her weeping, were seen as an expression of some pre-verbal construing.

We have all developed constructs during the very early days of our lives. Those designed to deal with our experiences when we were babies are 'core constructs' and are largely to do with dependency. We depended on others for our very existence. Most of us dispersed these dependencies on to other people and institutions as we grew older. But Trixibell seemed not to have done this. As she grew older and older her need for love and caring was never satisfied because she had never learned to depend on others for it. She only wanted it from her mother – who was never able to provide it.

This is an example of the nature of a transitive diagnosis. It represents a possible bridge between the past, the present and the future. It is also only a hypothesis to be tested out – it is a starting point.

Trixibell also had problems with migraine headaches. Such 'psychosomatic symptoms' can also be viewed as expressions of dependency and core, pre-verbal construing which cannot be communicated in any other way. The headaches or the stomach ulcer, or whatever the pre-verbal somatic expression is, are experienced now as they were originally. Young Trixibell, when feeling herself to be rejected by her mother, could well have become very tense which, in turn, may have led to a headache. On the other hand, it could be viewed as a dependency gesture, a calling out for love and sympathy. Now, in adult life, when feeling unloved, or wanting love, this same bodily feature is again experienced.

As we stressed in Chapter 1, Kelly's view of the process of construing is virtually identical to the notion of experiencing. We also pointed out that he does *not* think it useful to divide the person into separate parts of perceiving, thinking, feeling and so forth. Construing does not have to be in words. The person who is in deep meditation, with no words in the world he is experiencing, is still actively construing. But he is using another subsystem. The person absorbed in a piece of music is very actively construing – the music would have no sense otherwise – and yet that person is unlikely to have words going around in his head to describe what he is hearing.

So Trixibell had very different experiences when she was asked to 'get into' that other world of 'feeling'. It was as if her intellectual (verbal) subsystem of construing had little or no way of communicating with her feeling (non-verbal) subsystem.

If pre-verbal construing is hypothesised as being involved in the client's complaint, the counsellor knows he will have an uphill struggle. In particular, he has to consider the nature of the counselling relationship he will be expected to embark on. As a female, middle-aged counsellor I (Fay) had to work out very carefully what my role in relation to Trixibell should be. What do I have to beware of doing so as not to be cast as 'like my rejecting mother'?

Much pre-verbal construing does not involve such core issues. Some construing, developed in early life, has just never been 'updated'. We know that pre-verbal construing is involved by our sometimes irrational behaviours or body responses to otherwise innocuous situations. A chance remark sends the blood rushing to our cheeks.

There is an important distinction to be made here between Freud's notion of the unconscious and Kelly's construing at low levels of awareness. The principal difference is that, for Freud, it is psychic energy that 'pushes' the unconscious thoughts, images or whatever into consciousness. Kelly has no such principle as psychic energy. As Don Bannister (1977) said, Kelly did not find it useful to look at us all 'as if' we were hydraulic systems. We construe an event at a particular level of cognitive awareness because it is at that level we can make most sense of the event confronting us. We will be talking more about Kelly's approach to 'unconscious' construing when we talk of his views about transference (see Chapter 5).

Submerged poles of constructs   If pre-verbal dependency or core construing are likely to be involved, the counsellor needs to be alert for submerged poles of constructs. These are constructs in which the opposites have never been elaborated – they have little or no meaning. In that sense, only part of the construct is available to be consciously explored. All constructs have two ends or poles. One pole says how certain things are similar to each other and the opposite pole says how they are thereby different from other things. Normally it is the contrast end that is submerged. Trixibell saw herself as someone whose love was always rejected although she had so much to give. It was hypothesised that the opposite pole 'someone whose love is *accepted*' was very poorly elaborated.

Trixibell knew about rejection. In fact it seems likely that she went out of her way to ensure she received it. What she did not seem to know was how to construe being loved. This prevented change because we cannot be something we cannot construe.

An important question for counselling was: 'What would Trixibell do with a counsellor whom she could not *make* reject her?' Counselling is often a matter of helping the client deal with such submerged poles of constructs.

A most useful question in counselling can be 'what is my client *not* doing by behaving as she currently is?'. Seeking meaning in the opposites of what a client is saying, seeking those submerged poles of constructs, seeking those poles of constructs that have yet to be elaborated, there lies a great wealth of knowledge about the private world of our client.

Suspension   Sometimes changes in the construing of events happen which result in some experiences being 'left out in the cold'. The reconstruing has resulted in there being no way in which the event or experience can be accommodated in the realignment of the construing system. This event or experience is said to be 'suspended'. It remains so until such time as further reconstruing takes place which places it once more within the range of convenience of the constructs. Kelly equated the suspension of aspects of our construing system with forgetting.

Both the elaboration of submerged poles of constructs and the sudden availability of previously suspended events or experiences can produce what looks like 'insight'. Kelly defined insight as occurring when the client comes to adopt the counsellor's pet constructs. He was not keen on the usual meaning given to insightful experiences. He preferred to see them as the client's awareness of an experience not previously consciously available to him. Perhaps the reappearance of an event hitherto *suspended*.

Luke had one such experience. His face lit up when a childhood memory came back to him with obvious vividness. When a child he had a playmate – the squire's son. Luke's father was a farmer on land owned by the squire. There they were, these two children, going into the village shop. 'Two pennyworth of bullseyes, please,' says squire's son. Motherly shopkeeper hands them over and pats squire's son on the head, saying, 'And how are we today, Master John?' Squire's son makes an appropriate reply. Motherly shopkeeper turns to Luke and says: 'And what do *you* want?' Luke was not previously able to relate this memory to his desperate desire for respect in adult life – which, in turn, was related to his stammer.

'Ahha' experiences can work wonders for clients or can confront them with anxiety and threat that is unacceptable. The counsellor must be sure that the exploration of the implications of the insight do not exceed the client's ability to keep a grip on things. The client needs to be able to ensure that each implication can be made sense of and slotted into her existing construing system.

Construing in Transition

We keep coming back to this central point, that feeling and thinking are not separate entities but all linked together in what Kelly means by construing. To quote Kelly once more on the subject: 'The classic distinction that separates these two constructs [emotion, cognition] has, in the manner of most classic distinctions that once were useful, become a barrier to sensitive psychological inquiry' (Kelly, 1969b: 140).

Kelly integrates emotional experiences within his theory by seeing them as an awareness that our construing system is in a state of transition or an awareness that it is inadequate for construing the events with which we are confronted. Inevitably, signs that our client is aware of such states of transition will form an important part of our formulation (diagnosis) of the problem.

We must be careful, however, about imposing our own personal meaning of emotion on to someone else. If we do we may be guilty of misunderstanding them. Just as the imposing of traits on to others stifles individuality, so may the imposing of emotional labels. For instance, Helen Jones (1985) argues that we should not use the term 'depression' to describe someone's state. Every person who says they are depressed will, when listened to, provide their own idiosyncratic picture of the experience. This does not mean that there is no common denominator among all the 'depressions', just that the realities personally experienced may differ.

Although we shall be looking at each of these transitional states in turn here, they inevitably overlap.

Anxiety   This is an emotion we probably all think we can recognise and experience as something that very definitely exists and is different from what goes on in 'the mind'. Kelly links the two by suggesting that anxiety is experienced whenever we are *confronted by events which we find difficult to interpret or predict*. Anxiety is thus an inevitable companion of change. For whenever we put ourselves into a new situation, we *must* be faced with new events, some of which we are likely to have difficulty construing.

Anxiety means we cannot predict the outcome of our own actions nor the actions of others. We may not have met an event anything like this before and we do not know what we should do or even how we might think about it. Kelly points out that anxiety is by no means necessarily a bad thing: 'from the standpoint of the psychology of personal constructs, anxiety *per se*, is not to be classified as either good or bad. It represents the awareness that one's construction system does not apply to the events at hand. It is, therefore, a precondition for making revisions' (Kelly, 1955: 498; 1991: Vol. I, 367).

Cindy Lou (in the musical *Carmen Jones*) cries out at the pain of being faced with chaos when she discovers that Joe no longer wants her: 'I's like a leaf that's lost her tree.' With involvement of our whole being, it becomes clear that this is far more comprehensive than simply an 'emotional experience'.

Rose is waiting for her child at the school gates. It is later than usual and most of the other children have gone. John is often the first to appear, rushing out of the door with his coat half on. Time goes on and there is still no sign of him. Rose moves towards the main door to search for him and realises that it has already been locked. What has happened? Where is he? What should she do now? Rose cannot make immediate sense of what is happening. As well as this great anxiety, she probably experiences threat.

Threat   Threat is defined as *the awareness that we are facing imminent, comprehensive change in our core-role construing*. We see that the events confronting us may result in considerable change in those areas of our construing we guard most carefully – those to do with our notion of 'me' and 'I'.

Threat is an ever-present issue in any successful counselling – for we are asking the client to face precisely that which threatens – change in how they construe themselves. What counsellors sometimes see as resistance is often the client's way of dealing with threat. The stutterer who has been progressing towards fluency extremely well suddenly 'relapses' and gives up his newly established fluency for the old familiar stuttering speech. He may well have seen himself *becoming* a fluent person with the accompanying realisation that he has little idea of what sort of person that is going to be. Best to return to where the world is understandable and predictable – however undesirable that world may be.

John's failure to meet his mother at the school gates aroused not only anxiety (the inability to give meaning to the event) but also 'an awareness of imminent comprehensive change' in her core construing of herself as a good mother. Returning home and telephoning friends to see if he was there her whole sense of herself in relation to him began to be called into question: 'Am I the sort of mother who does not look after my child properly?' Such threatening and unpredictable situations can also give rise to guilt.

Guilt   Guilt occurs whenever we see ourselves behaving in a way that is *not like me*. *We are dislodged from our core-role structure.* The definition of guilt goes well beyond self-blame. In fact, guilt can occur without any conscious self-blame at all. Retirement for a counsellor can produce dislodgement from the core role of being a counsellor, as can long illness or a disfigurement in any active person.

Rose experienced anxiety and threat followed by guilt when she found out that John had left school on his own and had been knocked down by a car on his way home. She came for counselling. The guilt (the dislodgement of her 'self' from her core role as a mother) was profound. She had lost an important part of her sense of self.

Clara, who sees herself as very thrifty and values this quality, will experience guilt if she goes out and spends a large sum of money on a dress. Part of her core structure is about being thrifty, and thrifty people do not go and pour money out on themselves for no good purpose.

Kelly's definition of guilt is a good example of the value-free nature of personal construct psychology. The successful confidence trickster will experience guilt were he ever to feel sorry for a potential victim and let him off the hook. He would see himself as dislodged from the core structure of someone who is above such weaknesses.

Sometimes the counsellor perceives these states in the client straight away and their effects on the person's view of themselves is clear. At other times, it takes a little longer to clarify. George was feeling vaguely 'ill' and depressed. He was about to retire from teaching, which he had not enjoyed in the last few years and was looking forward to his 'freedom' and to all the things he meant to do with his time. Only after some elaboration of how he saw the coming event did it emerge that he had no clear picture of himself as 'not a teacher'. He was threatened by a kind of emptiness. Detailed plans and predictions relating to his new life helped to overcome his current anxiety and the experience of dislodgement when the time came.

Hostility   Whereas Kelly's definitions of emotions are based on *an awareness* of our construing of the world, hostility and aggressiveness are concerned with *action*.

Hostility is *the continued effort to extort validational evidence in favour of a type of social prediction which has already been recognised as a failure.* If we do not like the evidence we are receiving from our actions (we are experiencing invalidation from our experiments), we have three courses of action open to us. We can agree that our predictions were not good in the first place and we need to reconstrue; we can think we did not really read the evidence properly and so repeat the experiment; or we can try to 'cook the books'. In this last-mentioned course of action we extort evidence that proves we were right all along – we act in a hostile manner.

The person who stutters, and finds he is rushing towards his desired position – being fluent – at too fast a pace, returns to the known, familiar, old self. He extorts evidence to show that the changes he was experiencing were not really there. He will give many examples of how situations which the counsellor construed as signs of improvement were really just coincidences, or had unique qualities which would mean they could never occur again. He convinces himself that he is clearly still a stutterer.

There are four important features of hostility: (a) the person is aware that they are in an impossible situation. It is chaotic and fraught with anxiety; (b) the person sees (at *some* level of awareness) that it is the result of social experiments they themselves are conducting; (c) the person tries to behave in such a way that his original anticipations are 'true' without having to change himself: '*The hostile person seeks appeasement rather than understanding*'; (d) a person's hostility may be resolved by behaving aggressively.

Luke, who stutters, is experiencing great anxiety even though his counsellor seems to be so pleased at what she calls his 'progress'. He knows, at some level of awareness, that he is in an impossible situation. When he is fluent with others he gets evidence which he cannot properly construe – he just does not know how to behave as a fluent person – it has too little meaning for him. He returns to stuttering in situations in which he was becoming fluent. He does not try to understand his anxiety, he wants confirmation that he is still really a stutterer.

Aggressiveness is the active elaboration of a person's perceptual field
We push ourselves actively forward into the unknown, confront new problems, expose ourselves to new anxieties and expand our horizons in specific directions. In some senses aggression is the opposite of hostility. It is a moving forward and outward rather than backward and inward.

On the other hand, they are often linked. The aggressive person tends to be restless, keeps on exploring; other people find themselves involved in these explorations. Others find they cannot keep pace, the scenery shifts just when they think it has become predictable. They become hostile by attempting to impose limits on the aggressive person by making any development conform to the original idea. Evidence for such hostility comes from such comments as: 'but surely the whole idea when you started all this was . . .'; 'but you said last year that . . .'. The aggressive person has moved on and left others behind struggling to keep up.

Dilation and Constriction

These are the terms relating to expanding of horizons and imposing of limits on construing. Their function is to reorganise our construing system in order to deal with incompatibilities.

The client who *dilates* his perceptual field may (a) behave aggressively and widen his areas of interest, (b) jump from topic to topic and see possibilities everywhere, or (c) start to see everything as being related to his problem. In its extreme form, dilation can be seen in the person in a manic state.

There is nothing good nor bad about dilation; just as anxiety and other transitional states can be useful or damaging, so can dilation. Dilation which takes place gradually as new avenues are explored can be very helpful. However, if it comes about too quickly, the person will create for himself events he cannot construe adequately – and so experience anxiety. If the client dilates too quickly and experiences anxiety, one course of action is to help him *constrict*. This helps him minimise any incompatibilities he may be experiencing.

Luke used constriction to reconstrue himself as someone who wished to be respected for what he held to be important and not go on just 'grasping at *any* opportunity at all to get some respect out of the person'. This reduced the incompatibility between seeing himself as someone who had qualities he would like others to respect him for and his need to find this respect for everything he did.

Constriction is one useful way of dealing with personal chaos and anxiety. It helps avoid incompatibilities and makes the world 'manageable by shrinking it to a size he can hold in his own two hands' (Kelly, 1955: 901; 1991: Vol. II, 241). Like all professional personal constructs, it can be both helpful and create a problem. If the constriction is considerable, the client may describe the experience as feeling 'depressed'.

Loose and Tight Construing

For Kelly himself, one of the most important constructs in his theory for counselling is the *tight–loose* dimension. This is to do with our ability to make predictions. It is fundamental to the process of change – with the emphasis on the word 'process'.

In tight construing we make our predictions in an unvarying way. We know precisely what we are about. Events are consistently construed (predicted) on the same pole of the construct each time it is used. A person who today construes Susan as sulky as opposed to open construes her the same way tomorrow. Someone who is construing people in a loose fashion might see Mark as sulky today and as open tomorrow.

Poetry is a form of loose construing, as is dreaming. Both have strands of meaning very loosely knit together. Clients have very often tightened their construing in an attempt to deal with the increasing chaos in their world. It is an attempt to maintain at least some predictive stability. If 'tight construing' is part of the counsellor's transitive diagnosis, then the counsellor will try to encourage the client to loosen the bonds. The movement from tight to loose and back again is the basis of the Creativity Cycle, which is fundamental to the whole process of change.

The Cycles of Change

As we mentioned briefly in the first chapter, Kelly describes three cycles that are central to the change process. These are to do with experience, creativity and decision making. One of the complexities of viewing the person as an integrated process is the inevitable interrelationship between the theoretical constructs used. It could not be otherwise if we do not want to get back to the discrete chapter-heading model of the person in whom *learning* is different from *emotion* and different again from *perception*.

Thus, the three cycles of change overlap to some extent. The creativity cycle accounts for our originality, but our original thought may well precipitate us into wanting to take action which moves us into the decision-making (CPC) cycle. These, in turn, can lead us into the cycle of experience. However, there are fundamental differences between them which far outweigh their similarities.

The experience cycle   Here we are giving the bare bones of the cycle; the flesh will be put on in Chapter 7 where it is discussed in action.

The experience cycle has five phases. First there is *anticipation*. The person looks forward to what is to come. As Epting and Amerikaner (1980) remind us, this need not be at a cognitive level of awareness at all. Our anticipations may be at a gut level of fear or excitement. The second phase consists of *commitment* or self-involvement, where the person is open to experimenting with a new event. Next comes the *encounter* with the event. There the experience is fully construed at every level. And this

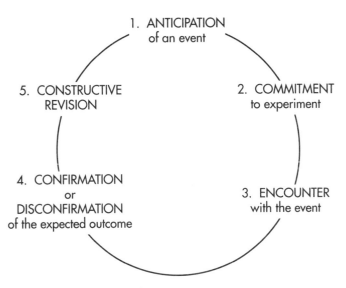

FIGURE 3.1 *The experience cycle*

will bring with it either *confirmation* or *disconfirmation* of the expected outcome. In the light of this the final stage of *constructive revision* will need to be undertaken. It may be that our anticipations will be largely confirmed, it may be that we have to look afresh at some long-held theory about ourselves. Whatever the outcome, there will be some degree of change. The person will never be quite the same again.

The creativity cycle　The fundamental nature of this cycle is its description of the process of change as being one of movement from tight to loose then loose to tight construing and so on *ad infinitum*. Sometimes the client is 'stuck' in one phase of the cycle or the other and is unable to move. We all need to tighten aspects of our construing at times and to loosen at others. Some people are more inclined to tighten, others to loosen. We would emphasise that this is not a trait. A person is not a 'tight' construer or a 'loose' construer. Everyone views aspects of their worlds from a tight perspective and other aspects from a loose perspective; also, everyone changes how they view things on a time dimension. What we are saying here is that we may have problems if we are locked into one mode only. We then have problems dealing with our world from the other perspective. We cannot be creative.

Mollie was having trouble with her neighbours. They kept her awake with their late hours and noisy ways and she felt she was becoming ill with fatigue and frustration. I (Peggy) discovered that she had some very tight construing about neighbours. You did not complain because they would only want to pay you back. You did not tell them of your distress because they would mock you. And, anyway, these neighbours were 'not a very good class of person' and such people were 'insensitive' and 'careless'. It took some loosening for her to contemplate dealing with the situation at all. Could she see an alternative to complaining or off-loading her distress which might have a better outcome? And, if she could, could she contemplate a response from them which was other than insensitive and careless?

It emerged that she hardly knew the family at all, preferring to keep herself to herself. It was suggested, therefore, that she might begin by talking to the mother, who seemed the least objectionable. She bravely stopped to talk to her one day and, to her surprise, found that she too had troubles of her own. One of her sons was ill and her husband was likely to lose his job. When Mollie expressed her sympathy, the other woman asked her how she was and whether she was lonely in the house all by herself. This led her to mention the fact that she slept rather badly, and she felt able, tentatively, to broach the subject of slamming doors and loud music. To her relief, her attempt at negotiating rather than complaining bore fruit and things improved.

Her construing loosened to the extent that although she still saw that some neighbours were clearly vengeful and mocking, insensitive and uncaring, others were not. They could also be friendly and have problems of their own. It was clear from the way she spoke of developing relationships with these neighbours and others that reconstruing people as a whole involved her in a process of loosening, then tightening, then loosening again as old theories were challenged and revised.

Someone who, in contrast, has difficulty in tightening his construing when appropriate will have a different kind of problem when it comes, say, to relating to others. Jim was such a person. When he tried to describe how he saw others and himself he immediately cast doubt on many of the conclusions he came to. He saw most people as varying between the poles of his constructs to an alarming degree. He was not at all sure whether he could call himself 'honest' or 'devious' and his father floated around between the poles of 'strong' to 'weak', 'has a sense of purpose' to 'drifts'. We worked quite hard at establishing some slightly less varying predictions by having him record his own responses in a series of similar situations at work. There *was* a good deal of consistency in his behaviour and he was able to tighten up to some extent about what *he* was like. Gradually he became more able to find a consistent pattern in the behaviour and attributes of those around him. Again, this reconstructive process entailed ongoing cycles of tightening then loosening again as his experience of people brought new aspects of them to his attention.

In both these instances it will be seen that the person's own behaviour was involved in the process of reconstruing a situation. Behaviour is the way in which we test out our present understandings. In the first example, Mollie had to take some different action in relation to her neighbours; in the second, Jim needed to observe what he did to find the beginnings of clarity about himself. It cannot be stressed too often that the construing process is a total experience and change often begins when an experiment in taking some kind of action is undertaken.

The CPC cycle   This is the cycle of 'circumspection, pre-emption and choice' leading to the making of a decision – a process in which we are all involved in large or small ways a great deal of the time. In the circumspection phase, a person surveys all the issues which might be entailed in making a

particular decision. Pre-emption refers to homing in on the most important of these issues, and choice represents the moment when the person
decides which way to jump with regard to that issue. And, here too, difficulties with the process may be a major source of stress for many clients.

The problem can manifest itself mainly at two extremes: the person may
be stuck in endless circumspection, failing often to come to any conclusion about anything. Or he or she may leap into a decision impulsively,
without considering the implications of their actions. In sheer despera-
tion, some people circumspect for a very long time and can only make an
impulsive choice in the end. Thus the circumspection phase is suddenly
foreshortened.

The Dilemmas of Mary

Mary was under great stress, feeling herself to be at a crossroads in a
number of areas of her life: should she leave her safe but boring job and
risk putting herself on the open market in a very competitive field? Should
she at last buy a flat, instead of continuing to pay exorbitant rents? Should
she agree to marry her boyfriend? It was useless taking her through the
cycle on each issue 'as if' she had made one or other decision to see what
the outcomes looked like. There were serious disadvantages whichever
she chose. If she left her job she would lose the security of a very good
income and she might not find enough work to keep herself as a freelance
designer. If she bought a flat of her own she saw it as dooming her to a
single life for ever and she might make a bad choice. If she married her
boyfriend she would no longer be lonely but her need for space would be
infringed. At this stage Mary seemed to be addressing these dilemmas
very much at a more concrete and cognitive level and to be out of touch
with any feelings such issues might have aroused.

Only by looking at the deeper, more superordinate, dilemmas preventing her from taking action were we able to make sense of the implications
of any of her decisions. From a child she had had great difficulty in trust-
ing her own judgement as all decisions were made for her by her mother.
She had never been allowed to make mistakes and to do so was a horrible
prospect for her. She had little trust in people's feelings for her or hers for
them – again largely due to the inconsistency of her parents' attitude
towards her. One minute they showed almost suffocating concern, the
next they showed no interest at all in what she did or felt. She had also
found that the achievement of anything she felt strongly about, whether it
was a relationship, some material thing she wanted or an experience she

longed for, always ended in a great feeling of disappointment and flatness.

The first decision she was able to make was over buying a flat. She was able on further reflection to separate the issue of buying her own home *now* from any implications of being alone or married in the future. She chose to look at it purely practically. You can always sell what you have bought. It could be seen as 'a good investment'. She approached the problem of being so stuck in her job by beginning to offer designs elsewhere, to test the ground for a possible future move. The question of marrying her boyfriend was far more complex as the implications of such a commitment naturally remained very serious. She had a great deal more work to do in moving on from her relationship with her parents. She needed, in her relationships with friends, to develop the ability to see things as others see them (sociality). Above all she needed to allow herself to experience strong emotions without terror, before she could take such a step with any confidence.

The Impulsivity of Jeremy

Jeremy had a history of leaping into major decisions like a soldier going over the top in battle. He found circumspection both difficult and tedious. And, once again, it was important to look at some of his core role constructs before we could attempt any change. It soon emerged that he had great admiration for his successful father, who took enormous risks in business and, in fact, had been a paratrooper during his earlier army career. The contrast pole to 'risking all' was 'stagnation'. The opposite of 'counts every penny' was 'leads a full life'. Jeremy himself had been ill for much of his childhood and regretted his physical 'weakness'. He seemed determined to make up for it by daring acts in work and even in relationships, where he both confronted those who offended him and declared undying love at first meeting to those he found attractive. In addition, he was continually in debt from one failed business venture or another which he had entered into with great enthusiasm but little thought.

He voiced his fear of having to become boring and cautious in order to change and stay out of trouble and approached the exploration of his way of doing things with some trepidation. We were looking dubiously at the possibility of his finding satisfaction in 'calculated risks' when his father unwittingly provided a useful model. They were talking about some successful coup he had made in business a short time previously and his father happened to describe how much work he had put into predicting the outcome of his decision. This led to his father also talking for the first time about the training and care involved in preparation for his feats of 'bravery' as a soldier. Jeremy had assumed that all his medals were the result of sudden inspiration. But it emerged that his father seldom did anything without meticulous planning. He was shocked to begin with and his father was almost toppled from his pedestal for a while. But it caused him to ponder on other ways of taking control and going into action.

There was more to it than that, of course. Jeremy also had some quite negative constructs about his own abilities and value as a person, which seemed to stem from feelings of helplessness and dependency as a sick child. The rash decisions, particularly in relationships, had much to do with 'getting in first' before he was simply ignored. Some attention to sociality was important here as he had not considered that other people might want time before an acquaintance was precipitated into passionate friendship or proposed marriage. His desire to make money quickly from wild business projects also had to do with wanting to emulate his father and make his mark by affluence if nothing else. In fact, he had much about him which was both attractive and admirable and when he came to value the qualities which others valued in him he found it easier to stop and consider the possible outcomes of some of his actions and alternative ways of approaching both people and ventures.

How Does the Client See the Problem?

This, of course, is central to the whole personal construct approach. You start from where the person 'is'. This may well also include asking how others who are important to her see the problem. Are they basically sympathetic? Do they feel that the client should 'pull herself together'?

But there is another issue here. The counsellor has to decide where to make a start, for diagnosis is a step-by-step process. The first step may be dictated by the client. In the extreme case when a client comes to the initial session threatening suicide or homicide, there is little doubt where you start. You act as if he means it and take appropriate action. This may involve seeking other professional help, perhaps from a psychiatrist or the client's general medical practitioner.

Or the client may be complaining about severe, continuing vomiting or headaches and he may look ill. You may hypothesise that the client has some physiological disorder or a brain lesion which would take priority over how he was construing that disorder. If that were your diagnosis you would take the appropriate action. In neither case are you having to decide whether your client is a 'psychological case' or a 'medical case'. Even if the client *does* have a brain tumour, this does not make him exclusively or even predominantly a 'medical' case. The issue is how he can best be helped to deal with his circumstances at this point in time.

The problem as seen by the client may be very different from the way society or the counsellor sees it. For instance, there was the arsonist who freely agreed that he was setting fire to buildings – after all he was serving a prison sentence for his acts and had in the mean time become depressed. Interviewing did not elicit from him any more information than that. However, when investigations were made using forms of Kelly's assessment instrument, the repertory grid (see Chapter 4 for details), it became clear that he was actually punishing society and committing not arson, but acts of purification (see Fransella and Adams, 1966).

Another extreme example is the anorexic girl who says that she has no problem at all. Her weight is normal and it is only her parents and society who are getting worried. In such a context, the counsellor faces many complex issues. Some say that you can only intervene in such instances by treating the whole family. The practical issue from a personal construct perspective is how to help someone who does not want to be helped. Also, one faces the moral issue of whether one has the right to intervene in such instances (for a further discussion of this issue, see Fransella, 1985).

GAINS AND LOSSES ACCRUING TO THE CLIENT THROUGH THEIR PROBLEM

The personal construct counsellor knows that in all cases the gains for the client must outweigh the losses *or else the client would not behave in that way*. The counsellor considers gains and losses within the context of validation and invalidation of the client's experience. We have created ourselves and our world so that it makes the most sense to us at this point in time. Validation comes from having correctly anticipated an event and invalidation from being proved wrong in our prediction. The question is 'What is being validated for the client by behaving as he does?' For example, the arsonist who lights fires to purify the world. What invalidations is he receiving that mean he has to become *hostile* and 'make' his predictions work and so prevent everything getting out of control? That man saw himself as an upright, righteous person and may have been invalidated in this – perhaps the world was not seeing him as he saw himself. So he *had* to prove to himself that he really could influence events and contribute to the world's betterment. He *had* to make it work because otherwise the threatening prospect of having to reconstrue himself as someone who was not upright and righteous would have required too great a re-shuffling of his entire construing system.

Is there any way in which Trixibell's actions (see Chapter 2) can be seen as making up for the love she feels she does not get? It seems necessary for her to continue to be a person who loves so wholeheartedly and is consistently unloved in return. Does the client's phobia, by keeping her at home, prevent her from doing something unacceptable? It is not unknown for a phobic client to have the feeling that she would become promiscuous if she were ever to be able to move around unfettered by her phobia. What validations does the person who stutters get? He can at least predict successfully people's reactions to him.

We are arguing here that, from the personal construct psychology perspective, no one of us can change if the change results in our becoming a person we cannot understand (cannot construe) or can understand less well than we do from our current position – be that putting up with periods in prison; being continuously rejected because of the overpowering nature of our own love; stuttering rather than entering that unknown world of the fluent speaker; or being house-bound. This theoretical position is spelled out in Fransella (1972) in relation to stuttering.

LOOKING FOR AREAS OF MOVEMENT AND CONSTRAINT

We have described how we try to understand the client from the *client's* point of view, and our ways of construing the client's construing from the standpoint of the counsellor using a set of professional constructs. The first level of understanding allows us to communicate with the client, the second level allows us to formulate a tentative hypothesis concerning the nature of the client's problem. Now we need to work out a plan to progress towards the change which the client has been unable to make alone.

Few clinicians would argue, no matter what their theoretical persuasion, that anxiety does not play an important part in any counselling setting. In personal construct theory, anxiety is indeed something that inevitably accompanies change as we push forward our personal frontiers (*aggression*). For our aggression confronts us with events which we have not previously experienced (*anxiety*). By being aggressive we are also extending our perceptual field (*dilation*). One of the ever-present problems with a client is that he may have constricted his perceptual field so as to make the world a more manageable place.

In the planning stage of counselling, we therefore need to look out for existing areas of anxiety, aggression and constriction. In what contexts is the client *currently* being faced with events he or she cannot adequately construe? Colin is 13 years old. He always has to be taken everywhere by his mother because he will not go out alone. As is so often the case with children, areas of anxiety are clear. To be able to find his way around on his own just fills him with dread. One of the issues turned out to be that you might have to ask strangers the way if you get lost. And there is a family construct that says you do not speak to strangers; 'we don't do that'. Colin's world was a very constricted one. It was basically peopled by his father and mother and his teddy bears.

By constricting to this extent, Colin had been able to limit some of the (unknown) incompatibilities in his construing of the world with which he had been confronted. But within that constricted world there were examples of where Colin was extending its frontiers. He was showing aggressiveness in learning how to use a microcomputer. He loved learning something new and mastering it. He felt competent here and was doing something that neither his father nor his mother could do. Otherwise, it was fair to say that almost everything they could do he could not do.

One of the ways of tackling Colin's separateness from the world and from the people in it was to use this aggressiveness in the area of mastering skills. He thought it a good idea to take up cooking as a skill. For the first time he worked *with* his mother and came to master something at which *she* had previously been the sole expert.

SAMPLING TYPES OF CONSTRUCTION THE CLIENT USES IN DIFFERENT AREAS

Here we would be trying to see the themes in relation to context. For instance, does the client show guilt when talking about her role as career woman and mother? Does she show stereotyped (constellatory) construing or pre-emption (men are nothing but . . .) in relation to male chauvinism? Or is there hostility when talking about her failure so far to find anyone who can help her with her problem and loose construing when contemplating the future?

We are here after the 'feel' of the client's construing system rather than attempting to arrive at a global blueprint. We are after ideas about where the client has room for movement and where the client will resist any change and why.

Just as there are differing levels at which a person is aware of his construing, so there are differing levels of communication. Kelly asks the following questions:

Will the client confide?

Can he use words?

At what level of abstraction does he pitch his communications?

Can he act out his major constructs in the counselling room as well as talk about them?

Will he seek to validate his predictions against the responses of the counsellor?

If the answer is no to any of these questions, then the therapist (counsellor) is likely to have a rough way to go. (Kelly, 1955: 803; 1991: Vol. II, 173)

UNDERSTANDING THE CONTEXT WITHIN WHICH THE CLIENT MUST CHANGE

It would be foolhardy to assume that anyone can adjust to any situation. This is especially so when one is about to help a person make some fairly radical adjustments to life. During these early stages of forming a picture of the client, a picture must also be formed about the social context within which the client moves and breathes.

A client who already had her problem prior to her marriage may well have serious difficulties in getting support and validation from her husband. He has married her as she was – obese, or stammering, or agoraphobic or . . . Perhaps he construes fat women as happy, cuddly and good mothers whereas those who are slim are inclined to be cold and argumentative. He may not take too kindly to his wife's successful slimming programme. He may appear very supportive and concerned, but every week or so reward her for all her hard work by giving her chocolates.

SUMMARY

We have covered the most important professional constructs used in personal construct counselling and some of the issues into which you need to get an understanding. The first tentative transitive diagnosis will be formulated in these terms. We hasten to add that the diagnosis will usually include only one or two of these professional constructs; the others will have been filtered out as not relevant at this time to the client's predicament. You may, of course, be wrong! You will only know this when you have tested it out. If you are limited to only a few sessions with the client you will have to foreshorten the diagnostic period and take more of a gamble that you are on the right tack. But some personal construct formulation of the problem must be made by the counsellor before he or she takes that first audacious step towards interfering in someone else's life.

So far we have only given the theoretical perspective that the counsellor adopts. We now move on to describe some of the methods that can be used to gain some understanding of the construing of another person.

4

EXPLORING THE CLIENT'S WORLD

SOME AIDS FOR EXPLORING PERSONAL CONSTRUING

Since all procedures developed and used within the personal construct framework are aimed at exploring the client's ways of construing the world, they are techniques and not tests. This applies particularly to the repertory grid described later, but is also relevant to other methods. These methods are all available for use by the counsellor but are not mandatory. No one *has* to use a self-characterisation or pyramiding or a repertory grid.

However, the personal construct counsellor cannot start a counselling programme until he or she has a relatively clear understanding of why the client has a problem which cannot be worked on without outside help. This understanding comes from having a picture of the client's construing of their personal world.

There are three main reasons for using such techniques: (a) they provide the counsellor (and also the client) with a more precise picture of the client's system for construing the world than can normally be gained from answers to questions; (b) stemming as they do directly from the personal construct framework, they give indications of possible new avenues or alternative constructions for the client to explore; (c) because of their focused nature, they speed up the whole process of establishing the transitive diagnosis of the client's problem.

By emphasising that the early sessions are used to plan the counselling programme, Kelly gave them great importance. Trial and error methods were not for him. As we stressed in the last chapter, he thought it was extremely important for counsellors to have a precise idea of what they were about. For how else can you test anything out? When you embark on your counselling programme with the client you should be able to state what hypotheses you are testing. How else do you know whether or not you and the client are on the right tack? Of course the plan will change, often very radically, but the counsellor must have a plan. Inexperienced counsellors all too readily want to leap into a programme of action without having any clear idea of the consequences of that action *as the client will construe it*. Since the counsellor is a personal scientist, how can he test out the effects of the experiments he is asking the client to undertake if he has no clear idea of what those experiments actually are?

The Self-characterisation

This is one of Kelly's two forms of assessment designed to fulfil the principle 'if you do not know what is wrong with someone, ask them, they may tell you'. Peter was given the instructions along the lines suggested by Kelly:

> I want you to write a character sketch of Peter just as if he were the principal character in a play. Write it as it might be written by a friend who knew him very *intimately* and very *sympathetically*, perhaps better than anyone ever really could know him. Be sure to write it in the third person. For example, start out by saying, 'Peter is . . .'

Here is Peter introducing himself:

> Even though I may be regarded as Peter's best friend, I feel as if I hardly know him! This may sound strange, for I have known him a long time. Wherever he goes he seems an outsider. Everyone will say 'Hi Peter – how are you' but that is as far as it will go. He doesn't want to make 'small talk' and niceties just for the sake of making conversation. He never liked or likes to go about with the same people all the time and identify himself with a particular group of people.
> I think the reason or one of the reasons for the fact that Peter was a 'loner' was his college education. He was, I suppose, a fairly typical

student – minus long hair – he studied a catering course and it wasn't allowed and therefore didn't have much money.

I don't think Peter has got an enemy in the world. I've never known him to have an argument with anybody or not speak to anyone for any period of time. He is extremely easy going and mixes – if he has to – with all types of people. He seems to be quite lethargic at times even though he does like the 'simple' things in life and is quite happy to just let events happen and take their own course.

There are only a few specific ways of analysing such self-characterisations, but they are mainly valuable in indicating important personal themes and in giving a 'feel' of how the person sees themselves and their life.

There is an omission in Peter's account that is of particular interest. Peter came for help to overcome his stammer. Although it is fairly reasonable to hypothesise that his being a 'loner' is related to his speech problem, to have no mention of it is unusual. However, Kelly suggests that the first sentence may usefully be viewed 'as if' it were a statement of how a person centrally sees themselves now. We can immediately see that Peter has a problem of identity: 'Even though I may be regarded as Peter's best friend, I feel as if I hardly know him!'

Likewise, the last sentence in a self-characterisation may be looked upon as an indication of where a person sees themselves as going. Peter's last sentence gives cause for concern regarding his desire to change: 'He seems to be quite lethargic at times even though he does like the '"simple" things" in life and is quite happy to just let events happen and take their own course.' Peter, in fact, ceased keeping his appointments after three sessions.

There is an assumption with the self-characterisation that the client will choose to talk about things that have enough structure for him to make sense but also that he will also touch upon – however gingerly – areas in which he is uncertain.

The client's choice of topics will also give an indication of how he sees himself as distinguishable from others. If he thinks he is pretty ordinary in physical appearance, this is unlikely to be mentioned. Unless, of course, he is desperately concerned about being so ordinary, in which case that is likely to show up somewhere. The self-characterisation can provide very valuable data for the counsellor, and often for the client, when the client is asked to talk about themselves both now, with their problem, and later without it.

Here are extracts from Amir on himself as someone who stammers:

Amir was born in a very well known family in Asia. For the first three years he was very ill. Then his grandmother gave him some home-made medicine. That worked, but after that stammering started . . . At first Amir used to hit his foot on the floor to talk. So in his class he was very very shy. In his shyness he became weak in his studies. But he became very very good in games . . . One day a boy laughed at him, so he beat him up then everything was OK. At the age of ten he had another fight. So after that no boy laughed at him. They respected him a lot and he became the tough boy of his school. He did not interfere with others' affairs and liked to be alone at times . . . In college he was better. He started reading books (all kinds). In a *Reader's Digest* he came across he learned that if he holds a small pencil in his fist and press it and talk it will work. So he tried. It worked for some time. Then he left it (or forgot it) to do it every day. He also tried homeopathy treatment for some time. Then he started taking medicine for nerves. So it worked a bit. I think it made his nerves a bit weak too . . . So he has improved a lot now. He can talk to other people. He hopes to be better soon.

One thing to be noticed here is that there is no construct about movement in Amir's self-characterisation. He saw his stammer as dominating his life and believed it had been caused by his grandmother giving him some herbal cure when he was very ill as a young child. He has tried various types of cure, mainly medical ones.

If the first sentence is a statement of the person now, then he is not so much an individual as someone anchored in his history. If the last sentence gives an indication of where the person sees themselves as going, then 'He hopes to be better soon' gives little indication of any determination.

Amir's self-characterisation of himself as someone who stammers was five and a half pages long while the one to do with himself as a 'fluent speaker' consisted of five lines. It said: 'If Amir was a normal person, he would be a better person, better in his work and meeting people. He would be a better man. This is what Amir would be if he was normal.' Apart from its totally idealistic nature, it is not a recipe for living. It is also important to note that he changed the focus from 'Amir as a fluent speaker' to 'Amir as a normal person'. For change to occur he must be helped build up a detailed picture of his future self. So, for him, not only must there be a bridge, but there must also be a new home (being a normal person) for that bridge to link with. We never found out whether he would have been able to make this radical change as he went back to Asia to work in his father's business.

Barry is 23 years old and also complains of problems with speaking. But he does not stutter. He came via a dental department/speech therapy department/hypnotherapist. He had been refused help from two large institutions. He had a history of minimal brain damage and had a below average intelligence score. I (Fay) was not at all confident I could help where others had failed, but Barry seemed very eager to talk to someone.

Apart from finding out a bit about his speech problem, I asked him if he would write a character sketch for me. He said he would try. But he never did produce one because it soon became clear that his problem, as he saw it, was that he could barely read and write and he wanted help with this. To check this out I asked him to write me a short piece about something that had interested him recently. He wrote: 'To day Sam Plade Bool. Fhrs he was the Picea. Then he Plade Kecher. At furst he Got to Bat. When he run he fel and Got a small Kut on his Chin. But he had a lot of fun.'

So instead of trying to hear about him on paper I asked him to tell me about himself into a tape-recorder. He chose to give me a detailed account of his work as a packer with a large firm. There was nothing very surprising contained in the account but it showed clearly that he could speak without much difficulty when he was interested in what he was talking about and, I hypothesised, when someone took the trouble to listen to him.

The self-characterisation does not have to be written down on paper for the basic idea of 'if you want to know what is wrong with someone, ask them, they may tell you' to be of value. Children will quite readily talk about themselves in the third person. Nor does it have to be something that is only given at the very beginning of counselling. It can be used as a basis for a reconstruing programme as will be seen in the account of Lisa in Chapter 6. It can be used to help the client see how far he or she has 'moved' during the counselling period. He may be asked to write a sketch of himself when he started out on his counselling. It can be used to monitor changes that seem to have taken place in the client's view. In fact, the self-characterisation can form the basis of the entire counselling programme (for example, see Fransella, 1981).

There was, for instance, Nick, who had written at the start of his counselling that:

beneath his public self there is a shy, uncertain and emotionally
insecure person who is pessimistic and skeptic toward life. Outwardly
he is attractive to people, especially women – they like his sense of the

absurd and frivolity. It is an impression that Nick has cultivated with some skill for, over the years, he has discovered that it provides the best means to protect a genuinely vulnerable and sensitive nature.

At the end of the ten contracted sessions he wrote:

> Nick can now tolerate his own company. This is probably the most important thing to say about him now. A few weeks ago, even one evening alone would have been difficult for Nick to face. Now he can face even a week or more days alone without worry. More than anything else this reflects a much stronger sense of self – a security that does not require recourse to being in company simply for the sake of company . . .

The Client's Construction of his Life Role

This can be based on the client's self-characterisation, but it need not be. It also goes further than the self-characterisation. Essentially it concerns becoming aware of how the client construes his biography. While 'no man need be a victim of his biography' we may become a victim of how we *construe* that biography. What does the client consider to be the most important events in his past? What meanings do these events have for him? As you will now be aware, this is not to say that it is the events that have pushed the client to where he is, but the interpretations he has placed upon his experiences. What is the thread of meaning that holds his experiences together? How will future events be added to this collection? The basic question becomes: 'how does my client construe his life role?'

The repertory grid can be introduced here. Since, in personal construct terms, a role is a course of activity played out in the light of our interpretation of other persons, we cannot hope to understand how a client construes his life role without learning something about how he construes other people. As you will see, the repertory grid is well suited to this purpose.

Repertory Grid Methods

This method was originally designed by Kelly to apply numbers to the relationships between the constructs, as well as to explore more precisely a client's 'repertoire' of those constructs. Mathematical and statistical procedures are not essential to derive useful information from a grid.

Much of interest can be gained from the elicitation procedures and from the raw data that make up the completed grid.

The best known way of getting a glimpse of another person's construing is to listen to them and watch them. In the first meeting with a client, this is usually all one is doing. However, sometimes it is necessary or desirable to move more quickly and more systematically.

Eliciting the elements   In order to create a grid you have to have something to put into it; in jargon terms, you have to have some constructs and some elements to be construed by those constructs. The choice of elements is at least as, if not more, important than the elicitation of constructs. *The elements have to be within the range of convenience of the constructs.* It is no use asking your client to apply his constructs to different types of paper if those constructs are to do with personal relationships.

Let us suppose you are interested in how your client construes those with whom he works. You first ask him to name some – about eight to ten is usually enough. These should include a range of people along dimensions that seem to be important: for example, some bosses, some subordinates, some men, some women, some older, some younger, some liked, some not liked. As simple arithmetic shows, if you had two of each of those the number of *elements* would be 16. This would normally be too many. It is not that they are necessarily unimportant, but that it would take too long for the client to complete the later grid. Choices have to be made according to the aims of the elicitation – which of these element groups are most important for the task in hand? The point here is, and it applies to everything to come, that there are no hard and fast rules about creating a grid. Grids are techniques that you can use creatively to answer your own questions. In practice, it is sometimes useful to write down each name on separate small cards.

For those who are interested in exploring new methods, there are several computer programs available which 'talk' the client through the triadic elicitation process. Others feel that insights into the client's world can be gleaned simply by observing how the client goes about the business of completing the tasks the counsellor is setting him.

Procedures for eliciting constructs   Kelly describes several ways of formally eliciting constructs from people, and other methods have been evolved since. Just as this book is not designed to make the reader a trained personal construct listener, counsellor or repertory grid mechanic, so it will not give you enough information about these procedures for you to feel totally happy in using them. But it is to be hoped that you will get enough of the sense of the procedures to enable you to try some of them out.

ELICITING BY USING TRIADS   This is a very straightforward procedure. Take three of your client's element cards and ask if there is *any important way in which two of the elements are alike and thereby different from the third*. A reply might be that two are *overbearing*. If the client does not automatically give you the opposite of this likeness, ask 'What would the opposite sort of person be to an overbearing person?' You go on in this way using different sets of three cards either until all triads are exhausted, or until your client keeps repeating herself, or until you think you have a reasonable sample of constructs – perhaps one construct from each of ten triads. The ultimate choice is yours.

Since all constructs are theoretically organised into a *system* and so have links with each other, it is possible to follow through this network both to more and more abstract constructs – *laddering* – and to more and more concrete constructs – *pyramiding*.

LADDERING   Laddering is very much a skill or 'art form'. It requires sensitive ears attuned to hear what the person is saying behind the words. This involves both credulous listening and the subsuming of the other's construing. Often you are asking the person to consider aspects of their way of understanding the world which they have never thought of before. It is here that you need to be especially alert so as to hear when the person is saying they are beginning to feel uneasy about the route the explorations are taking. The illumination that often comes with laddering can be both exciting and interesting as well as alarming and threatening.

Laddering consists no more and no less than of asking the question 'why?' The person first is asked which pole of a given construct he or she would prefer to describe them. For instance, Roger's choice was between the one pole of his construct being *someone who could just 'be'* or the opposite pole being someone who *wears a mask*. In this case Roger said he would prefer to be someone who could just *be*. Now the 'why?' question. 'Why would you rather be someone who can just *be* rather than someone who *wears a mask*?' The question can be phrased in many ways. 'What are the advantages for you . . .?' or 'Why is it important for you . . .?' The aim is to develop a conversational style rather than simply to repeat the question 'why?' in a rather monotonous way as the person climbs the ladder of their construing system. Once again, there are no hard and fast rules. It is a skill which most people only acquire after some considerable practice.

Roger said he would rather just *be* because *you don't get caught out if you are being yourself* whereas if you are *wearing a mask* you *have to be on your guard to maintain consistency*. While it is important to write down precisely what the person says – otherwise you risk imposing your own meanings on what the client is trying to convey – it is also often necessary to use a shorthand. For Roger's rather lengthy reply we agreed on the shorthand *don't get caught out* as opposed to *on guard to maintain consistency*. The next question was: 'But why is it important for you to be the sort of person who *does not get caught out?*' He replied: 'Because you are *in control then.*' Since it is always important to keep an eye on that opposite pole of the construct my next question was: 'Whereas if you have to be on your guard to maintain consistency you . . .? He replied: '*You are controlled.*' Next came: 'And what are the advantages *for you* to being the sort of person who is *in control?*' 'You are *free from threat*. If you are not in control you feel in a constant state of tension. It is awful to feel like that.' He, like many others, got the idea of giving the opposite pole of the construct he was talking about.

Ladders typically take you into the areas of the most superordinate constructs. These are constructs to do with what life is all about; life and death issues; religious constructs; what someone feels they cannot do without. You get right into a person's basic system of values. It is perhaps not surprising that people's superordinate constructs are those that are most resistant to change.

PYRAMIDING This procedure, first described by Landfield in 1971, involves asking the person successively to 'climb down' their construct system to more and more concrete or subordinate levels. The questioning asks for more specific details of the construct. For example, 'What kind of a person is someone who is introverted?' The answer may be *hard to get to know* versus *easy to know*. The next question might be 'What kind of person is someone who is hard to get to know?' The same type of questioning then takes place with the opposite pole of the construct. In schematic form it looks like this:

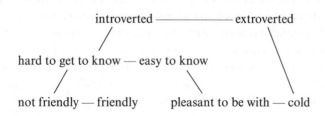

To get to specific behaviours you can ask: 'How do you know when a person is *cold*? What do they actually do that makes you think they are *cold*?' One such answer might be *they look at you without blinking.*

This procedure can be particularly useful when you have a client who has specific interpersonal problems. You may want to do what in behaviour therapy terminology would be 'social-skills training'. For instance, having found out what the personal meaning of being cold is for that person, you could use role play to help the client look at various ways in which she, and others, may cope with a *cold* person. If the problem is that it is others who think the client is cold, then the same procedure can usefully be used to specify what, in her behaviour, others are construing as *cold*.

The ABC Model

In 1965, Hinkle extended Kelly's theory by talking about the meaning of a construct being seen only in the network of what it implies and what is implied by it. That is, one only knows what *cold* means for a person by finding out what being *cold* implies and, conversely, what is implied by being cold. Being *cold* may imply being *stand-offish*, but being *stand-offish* need not necessarily imply being *cold*. It may be possible to be *stand-offish* in an uncaring way that is neither *warm* nor *cold*. The implications of constructs need not be reciprocal, as will be seen later in the *implications grid*.

Tschudi (1977) elaborated Hinkle's idea of 'implicative dilemmas' into a procedure he has called *the ABC model*. In 1984 he published an analysis he had carried out with Sigrid Sandsberg of therapy with a client (described in Bannister and Fransella, 1986). This client had a phobia about travelling and telephones. He had a year of behaviour therapy, which was successful. He was able to travel and to use the telephone without fear. However, far from being pleased, the client was totally dejected. He saw the whole exercise as pointless. He had nowhere to travel to and no one to ring up. He then had about two years of psychotherapy focusing on helping him establish relationships with his fellows. After this he was able to go anywhere he wanted and to visit his newly found friends, involving mainly superficial chit-chat with men, and joining various hobby groups. But he now pointed out that this was useless to him since what he really needed was a deep, passionate and intense sexual relationship with a woman.

Tschudi's ABC model goes like this:

A: the problem: a1 actual state: *can't use telephone or travel*
              a2 desired state: *can telephone and travel*

The client is now asked the disadvantages of a1 and the advantages of a2.

B: thus: b1 disadvantages of a1: *prevents social possibilities*
         b2 advantages of a2: *open for new social possibilities*

The next questioning elicits what it is that prevents movement. The client is asked for the advantages of the present state and the disadvantages of the desired state.

C: prevents movement: c1 advantages of a1: *hides lack of friends*
                     c2 disadvantages of a2: *will reveal lack of friends*

The problem then became redefined as:

A: the problem: a1 actual state: *lack friends*
              a2 desired state: *have friends*
C: prevents movement: b1 advantage of a1: *will hide lack of true love*
                     b2 disadvantage of a2: *will reveal lack of true love*

The problem is redefined once more:

A: the problem: a1 actual problem: *lack true love*
              b2 desired state: *obtain true love*

The ABC model of eliciting constructs can be highly informative for counsellor and client alike. However, it needs to be used with care and at the right time. It would at best be meaningless and at worst highly damaging to ask someone who had stuttered all his life for the advantages of stuttering and the disadvantages of being fluent in the first few sessions. If you hypothesise that the client will be unable to accept that there are advantages, then that is what counts and you do not embark on that path for the time being.

This underlines a cardinal rule in personal construct counselling – the counsellor only asks the client to undertake some experiment or makes some suggestion *if she is fairly sure that the client can make use of the outcome*. At the right time, however, the ABC model is not only a method of assessment but also plays a part in the reconstruction programme. For some clients it may well be used during the initial assessment interviews.

Mary was one such client. She was overweight – not enormously so, but enough to make her unhappy. She had no problem losing weight, but she always put it right back on again. Her ABC went like this:

desired state	*present state*
slim	fat
advantage	*disadvantage*
look attractive	look unattractive
disadvantage	*advantage*
likely to be raped	unlikely to be raped

Once that sequence of events has been identified, the next step became clear. Did she really mean this? Are all attractive girls raped? If not, how do they manage to avoid it? And so forth. Only when a dilemma has been put into words can it be explored.

But a word of warning is again necessary. The methods of pyramiding, laddering and the ABC model (particularly the last two) are skills that have to be acquired and have in-built dangers. If something is powerful for good it is also powerful for ill if misused. The inherent potential dangers in these procedures lie in what they may lead a person to understand about their own construing. A person may be happy seeing themselves as someone who *takes things as they come*. As they explore their system by, say, laddering, they may start to see that the path along which they are moving is going to end up with some notion that people who *take things as they come* are those who *have no commitment in life*. For this person, having commitment in life is extremely important. You may have inadvertently moved straight into a vastly important implicative dilemma of which the person has become consciously aware for the first time.

These methods of elicitation of constructs often provide sufficient information in themselves for an initial transitive diagnosis of the problem to be made. However, it is also often useful to 'go beyond the words' by creating some form of repertory grid.

Repertory Grids

This is a systematic way of helping the client look at his or her own construing. As just illustrated, the procedures for eliciting constructs from clients, for exploring the constructs' relationships with each other by laddering, pyramiding or using an ABC approach, all help the client along the path to reconstruction. The grid is a formal way of demonstrating the mathematical relationships between specific constructs and the things (elements) construed. Not everyone is at home with numbers and there is nothing that says a personal construct counsellor *should* use one with every client. Yet they can be of great value.

If you are going to use a grid to elicit data from your client, it is important how you prepare your client for this. In an analysis of some of George Kelly's therapy tapes, Bob Neimeyer gives us an example of how Kelly approached the matter with his client, Cal, whom he had previously seen for five sessions:

> Maybe today is a good time to do something more formal and less involving and less tension provoking. You remember I mentioned we might do kind of a formal exercise to give me some better understandings of how you see things. I don't think you'll find this particularly threatening; if you do, by all means tell me. (Neimeyer, 1980: 85)

One approach is to use a grid quite early on in the sessions if you think the client and you will both benefit from it. If you want to do this it is a good idea to state, as a fact, that you and the client will be involved in completing some fairly formal exercises to speed up the process of coming to understand how the client sees things. If the client has written a self-characterisation she soon starts to get the picture. When it comes to formal elicitation and laddering the client usually takes it in her stride. It is rare for a client to have any problems here since you are clearly dealing with issues central to her concerns.

Choosing the elements   Having decided that some form of grid would be useful, the first thing to decide is the type of elements to use. Typically, elements consist of role titles as originally suggested by Kelly. These are such things as 'a person I admire', 'a person who makes me anxious or uneasy', 'a person who has influenced me', 'a person I dislike', or any other title that seems appropriate for that particular client. But this is by no means a rule.

If there is a rule, it is that the choice of elements to be used in any particular grid will be determined by the purpose for which the grid is being designed. If you wish to investigate a person's construing of cars, the elements are likely to be various types of car; if the family is the focus for investigation then the elements are likely to be people who make up that family and perhaps members of other families for comparison purposes.

Grids with children may use dolls to represent family members or children whom the child knows at school. If self-identity is a problem, various aspects of the self may form the elements – 'me now', 'me in ten years' time', 'me as I would like to be' and so on. Sheila, for instance, had part of herself she described as 'a Victorian governess' and another part was her 'immoral self', so these were included among the elements.

Sometimes it is useful to design two grids – perhaps, as with the self-characterisations, one to do with 'me now, with my problem' and a second on 'me without my problem'. Two grids may be used to investigate a person's sexual orientation, one with all women as elements and the other with all men.

Elements may appear to the outsider as quite unusual, but they may be extremely important to the person concerned. As you will see in the example of a ratings grid to follow, Richard had included in his grid as elements the four toy soldiers which inhabited his 15-year-old world. Since he was also interested in war games, the Duke of Wellington and Lord Kitchener were also included.

One of the early grid studies (Fransella and Adams, 1966) looked at the construing of a man who had committed several acts of arson and was at that time in hospital because he was depressed. We were interested in how he construed setting fire to things and how this might change as the result of the psychiatric treatment he was receiving. We gave him eight different grids over a period of time. For some we used photographs of men as elements and for others people he knew. The important point to note here is that the patterns of constructs were very similar whether photographs of strangers or people he knew were used as elements. Theoretically this is what one would expect, but it is always important to demonstrate the validity of such expectations.

Elements can be situations. For instance, if you are interested in studying the relationship between a person's construing of a situation and the severity of his stuttering, it is useful to use elements of such descriptions as 'talking to a group of strangers', 'talking to one person I know' and so on (see the 'situations grid' in Fransella, 1972).

Ryle and Lunghi (1970) describe the use of a 'dyad grid'. In this the elements are relationships such as 'myself in relation to my father', 'my father in relation to me', 'my mother in relation to my brother' and 'my brother in relation to my mother' and so on. No matter what form of grid is to be used, the basic guideline about the elements is that they must be construable by and meaningful to the client and pertinent to the investigation in hand.

Eliciting the constructs Having chosen the elements, you can elicit a sample of the client's constructs as already described earlier in this chapter. It is important to remember that this is all you have, a sample of your client's constructs. It is useful to spare a few moments to ask yourself some questions about how your client dealt with the procedure. Did he have available a wide range of verbal labels for his constructs? Did words come easily to him?

We are going to give a few examples of how grids have been used to help personal construct practitioners in coming to understand the construing of a client (details of repertory grid methods and descriptions of different forms of grid can be found in Fransella and Bannister, 1977).

The first form of grid to be described requires the client to give ratings to each of the elements. This is not an intrinsically difficult procedure, but obviously there are a variety of ways in which a client may respond to it. Since this is all part of the data-gathering stage of the counselling process, it is useful to study how the client reacts to the procedure. For instance, is his assigning of construct labels to the elements done in a forceful way suggesting that he has a considerable amount of emotion invested in them? Although you are primarily embarking on a process of assessment, it should always be borne in mind that the client is being given the opportunity to examine his own construing system at close quarters. You should always be on the look-out for threats and anxieties during the administration procedure.

Ratings grids In this type of grid, each construct is treated as a scale and each element is given a rating on that scale. Quite often the scale goes from '1' to '7', but it can be longer if finer discriminations are thought desirable. A shorter scale of perhaps only three intervals is more suitable for children.

A standard procedure for administering a grid made up of ratings is as follows:

1　Write the name of each element on a separate card, with the element numbers on the front of the card in the top corner.
2　Present the first element to the client and ask him to give a rating to this element on the first construct. You will have decided whether the construct poles on the left side of the grid are to be '1' or '7'. It does not matter, all that matters is that you are consistent. In this grid, the left pole is '1' and the right pole '7'.
3　In the following example, Richard is first asked to think of his mother on the *intelligent–stupid* construct. He is told that a '1' means he thinks

she is extremely intelligent whereas '7' would mean he thinks she is definitely not intelligent; a '2' or a '6' would mean not quite as intelligent or as unintelligent as a '1' or a '7' would indicate; a '3' or a '5' means he thinks she is fairly intelligent or fairly unintelligent; and a '4' means he thinks she is neither one nor the other. The actual wording is not vital, all that is required is that the person gets the idea of what a rating scale is about. This first rating is entered in the top left cell of the grid. Richard rates his mother as '3' on the *intelligent–stupid* construct.

	1	2	3	4	5	6	7	8	9	10 ...	17	
intelligent	3											not intelligent
worrying	3											carefree

The second construct, *worrying* versus *carefree*, is now used as the dimension through which to construe mother. Richard again gives her a rating of '3' – slightly on the worrying side. And so the ratings of his mother continue until all constructs have been used. The process is repeated with each element until the matrix of ratings is complete. Richard's completed grid is set out in Figure 4.1.

Of course, there is nothing to stop you from taking one construct at a time and using it to construe all the elements before moving on to the second construct. At the present time it is a matter of preference, there being no research indicating whether different results are obtained from the two different procedures.

Having administered your grid, there are many ways of analysing such a matrix of ratings, but it is usually found necessary to resort to one of the computer programs which analyse them into the principal ways in which the constructs and elements group together. There are several programs now available for microcomputers.

Before rushing off to the nearest computer, however, there are a number of things one can see from the matrix of ratings itself. For instance, it is of potential interest to see along the first row of ratings, that Richard gives no one a rating at the *not intelligent* end of the construct – all are to some degree *intelligent* except for one soldier who is neither one thing nor the other. The first question to be asked is whether this may be a submerged pole of the construct (see Chapter 3, p. 38). That is, perhaps Richard has never considered what it means for someone to be other than intelligent.

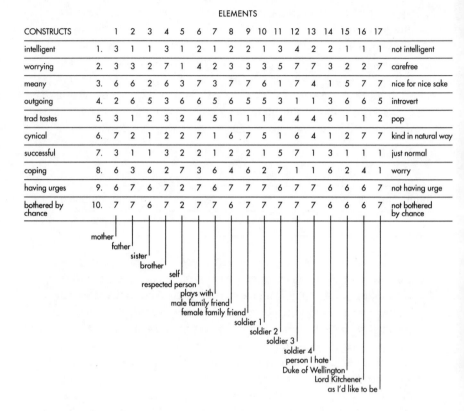

ELEMENTS

CONSTRUCTS		1	2	3	4	5	6	7	8	9	10	11	12	13	14	15	16	17	
intelligent	1.	3	1	1	3	1	2	1	2	2	1	3	4	2	2	1	1	1	not intelligent
worrying	2.	3	3	2	7	1	4	2	3	3	3	5	7	7	3	2	2	7	carefree
meany	3.	6	6	2	6	3	7	3	7	7	6	1	7	4	1	5	7	7	nice for nice sake
outgoing	4.	2	6	5	3	6	6	5	6	5	5	3	1	1	3	6	6	5	introvert
trad tastes	5.	3	1	2	3	2	4	5	1	1	1	4	4	4	6	1	1	2	pop
cynical	6.	7	2	1	2	2	7	1	6	7	5	1	6	4	1	2	7	7	kind in natural way
successful	7.	3	1	1	3	2	2	1	2	2	1	5	7	1	3	1	1	1	just normal
coping	8.	6	3	6	2	7	3	6	4	6	2	7	1	1	6	2	4	1	worry
having urges	9.	6	7	6	7	2	7	6	7	7	7	6	7	7	6	6	6	7	not having urge
bothered by chance	10.	7	7	6	7	2	7	7	6	7	7	7	7	7	6	6	6	7	not bothered by chance

mother
father
sister
brother
self
respected person
plays with
male family friend
female family friend
soldier 1
soldier 2
soldier 3
soldier 4
person I hate
Duke of Wellington
Lord Kitchener
as I'd like to be

FIGURE 4.1 *Richard's completed repertory grid*

If this were the case, Richard would have no option but to be *intelligent*. He would have no channel along which to move – we cannot move to where there is no meaning. There are two other explanations. It could be that he does have some meaning at the *not intelligent* pole of the construct, but all those used in the grid as elements are at the *intelligent* end of the construct. If the latter were the case, then any possible movement towards the *not intelligent* pole would produce overwhelming threat if not anxiety.

Looking at the ratings down column 5 it can be seen that Richard sees himself as very definitely *worrying* rather than being *carefree*, *cynical* rather than being *kind in a natural way*, again *worrying* rather than *coping* and, lastly, being *bothered by chance*. It is worthy of note that he is the only person rated as being *bothered by chance*. A check of ratings for how he sees himself (element 5) against those for how he sees himself ideally (element 17) shows that he does not want to be as he is.

We start to get a picture of a young person with some problems.

Many people like to stop at this stage and use the data collected so far to formulate a transitive diagnosis, and plan the first steps of the counselling programme. Others want to get the most they can out of the grid and so put it through some form of computer program.

The procedure used to analyse Richard's grid was one designed by Higginbottom and Bannister called GAB or 'grid analysis for beginners'. It basically gives the relationships between the ratings for each pair of constructs and then for each pair of elements. It shows, separately, how the constructs and the elements are closely linked together. These close linkages can be positive or negative. That is, the ratings in the rows 'intelligent' (construct 1) and 'successful' (construct 7) are pretty similar; the ratings, in fact, correlate +0.89 (the maximum correlation, perfect identity being +1.00). On the other hand, the ratings in the columns for the elements 'self' (element 5) and 'soldier 3' (element 12) are fairly dissimilar. Where there is a rating towards 1 in one column there tends to be a rating towards 7 in the other column. This results in a correlation of –0.76. With correlations, perfect similarity and perfect dissimilarity are equally related – it is just that one is +1.00 and the other is –1.00. The logic is that in each case you can predict with perfect accuracy what the second rating will be, given the first one. Most relationships between ratings will not be perfect and this is reflected in the correlation until such time that there is no possibility of predicting ratings, when the correlation will be zero.

The correlations above 0.50 are set out for both constructs and elements in Tables 4.1 and 4.2. That level of correlation is chosen as the point at which one can start to have some confidence that the relationship is too close to have happened by chance.

One aspect of this table is immediately striking. Element 5 has only one significant correlation with any of the other 16 elements in the grid. Element 5 is how Richard sees himself. The only way in which he sees anyone as being definitely like him is 'Soldier 3' and even that is a negative relationship. In the context of all those elements used in the grid, Richard knows himself because he is *not like* soldier 3. He does, however, know much better how he would like to be, as can be seen by the substantial number of significant relationships between 'as I'd like to be' (element 17) and the rest.

We can now look at the relationships between the constructs to see if

TABLE 4.1 *Significant correlations between the elements in Richard's grid*

Elements		1	2	3	4	5	6	7	8	9	10	11	12	13	14	15	16	17
mother	1.	X							0.64	0.83							0.69	
father	2.		X	0.73	0.67		0.77	0.65	0.85	0.75	0.90					0.98	0.76	0.69
sister	3.		0.73	X				0.91				0.66				0.69		
brother	4.		0.67		X								0.66	0.84	0.72			0.69
self	5.					X							−0.79					
respected person	6.		0.77				X		0.88	0.80						0.79	0.90	0.88
play with	7.		0.65	0.91				X							0.83			
male family friend	8.	0.64	0.85				0.88		X	0.94	0.94					0.85	0.97	0.77
female family friend	9.	0.83	0.75				0.80		0.94	X	0.86					0.72	0.95	0.67
soldier 1	10.		0.90						0.94	0.86	X					0.90	0.90	0.87
soldier 2	11.			0.66								X			0.85			
soldier 3	12.				0.66	−0.79							X	0.68				
soldier 4	13.				0.84								0.68	X				0.75
person I hate	14.				0.72			0.83				0.85			X			
Duke of Wellington	15.		0.98	0.69			0.79		0.85	0.72	0.90					X	0.77	0.67
Lord Kitchener	16.	0.69	0.76				0.90		0.97	0.95	0.90					0.77	X	0.73
as I'd like to be	17.		0.69		0.69		0.88		0.77	0.67	0.87			0.75		0.67	0.73	X

these offer any additional data which may help us understand the quandary in which Richard finds himself.

The first obvious feature of the construct correlation matrix in Table 4.2 is that Richard sees a number of intelligent people as worrying and people who worry have urges and are bothered by chance. If we look at these opposites we immediately see an implicative dilemma which Richard has got himself into. Carefree people (which is as he wants to be) are not intelligent, are outgoing, do not have urges and are not bothered by chance. The immediate apparent dilemma is that he cannot see himself as both intelligent *and* carefree and free from worry, not having urges and not being bothered by chance. But his ideal can separate them out all right. One hypothesis might be that he *has* to make worries for himself otherwise he will not be able to see himself as *intelligent* any more. One way of making worries could be by being obsessed by chance.

The grid is a tool that can 'get behind the words' on occasion or act as a hypothesis generator. These hypotheses can then be checked out with the client as appropriate.

A bi-polar implications grid   This is a modification (by Fransella, 1972) of the grid originally described by Hinkle in 1965. Hinkle was arguing that the meaning of any construct should be looked for in terms of what it implies and what implies it; so instead of using the constructs to construe elements, his implications grid compares constructs with each other. Fransella found his method far too cumbersome for general practical use and she had also become very interested in the opposite poles of constructs. So in order to study the implications of both poles of the constructs and make the administration simpler for a non-student population, she redesigned it. The bi-polar version looks at the linkages of meanings for each construct pole separately. The standard procedure is as follows:

1   Once again, each construct is written on a separate small card or piece of paper, with one pole designated 'a' and the other 'b'.
2   This procedure is repeated so that now you have two sets of cards.
3   Cut one set in half so that there is only one pole of a construct on each piece.
4   Lay the uncut cards out on the table in front of the client.
5   Select one pole of a construct from the half-cards.
6   Say something like: 'If all you know about someone is that they are X, what else, from all these things on the cards in front of you would

TABLE 4.2 Significant inter-construct correlations in Richard's grid

					Constructs							
		1	2	3	4	5	6	7	8	9	10	
intelligent	1.	X	0.59		-0.76			0.89				not intelligent
worrying	2.	0.59	X		-0.65				-0.64	0.53	0.51	carefree
meany	3.			X		0.52	0.82		-0.59			nice for nice sake
outgoing	4.	-0.76	-0.65		X	-0.60		-0.63				introvert
trad tastes	5.			0.52	-0.60	X						pop
cynical	6.			0.82			X					kind in natural way
successful	7.	0.89			-0.63			X				just normal
coping	8.		-0.64	-0.59					X	-0.57		worry
having urges	9.		0.53						-0.57	X	0.92	not having urge
bothered by chance	10.		0.51							0.92	X	not bothered by chance

you *expect* to find in that person?' It is imperative that the person understands that you are only interested in what qualities they would *expect* a person to have if they were, for instance, *boring*. You are not interested if they might or might not be *pompous*. You are only going to note it down if a *boring* person is *expected* to be *pompous*.

7 Let us suppose that the construct pole is 2b, then the row in the grid marked 2b is filled in with an asterisk whenever the person says that he expects a person to have that characteristic. In the example below, the client said he would *expect* a *careless* person to be 1b, 3a, 5b and 7a. The 'X's are simply indicating the diagonals.

		1a	1b	2a	2b	3a	3b	4a	4b	5a	5b	6a	6b	7a
	1a	x												
	1b		x											
	2a			x										
careless	2b		*		x	*					*			*

8 Since a person cannot 'expect' to find the opposite characteristics of a construct in the same person, the statistical analysis of this grid requires that a person does not say that *careless* people will be *expected* to be both 3a *and* 3b. This is a statistical constraint imposed on this grid.

The analysis provides information on the degree to which the entries in any pair of lines match or mismatch.

Nick was a teacher who had, for some considerable time, hidden his feelings from those around him. As expressed in his self-characterisation (see p. 60) he had feelings of depression. At about the third of his ten sessions he completed a bi-polar implications grid using the constructs elicited and laddered at his second session.

The first point to be made about Nick's grid is that the statistical analysis, itself, helped him enormously. I (Fay) showed him the computer printout – several pages of it – and pointed out that a lot of his constructs were highly related to each other. There was a great deal of structure in his construing. He paused for a while before saying that it was an enormous relief to see that because he had privately been worried that he was going mad.

The second point of value in the grid results was the suggestion that his identity lay in how he thought others saw him. That is, the only one of the 19 constructs in the grid to which 'like me in character' was related was 'as others see me'. But we know from his self-characterisation that people get a false impression of him: 'beneath his public self there is a shy, uncertain and emotionally insecure person . . .'. The opposite pole of the self-construct ('not like me in character') was related to 15 of the 19 constructs. He was clear about what he was *not*, but unclear about who he was. His grid was saying that those who do not have a clear notion of a self fear loneliness, are dependent and could be irresponsible. His dilemma was clear – he was living a lie.

Amir also completed an implications grid and it, too, showed structure. So much structure in fact that virtually all the constructs were related to each other. Very importantly from a counselling-outcome point of view is what was at the centre of the cluster.

As can be seen from the star-shaped diagram in Figure 4.2, the central construct pole is *stammerers*. It is as if his whole world were revolving around that feature of himself. But even more important than that, to be a stammerer was 'good'. People who stammer are like he would like to be, are intelligent, share their thoughts, are not likely to hurt people, are straightforward and frank, and so forth. Everyone was asking him to move to being a *non-stammerer*. But to move there would be to become a person who was a stranger to him – the only thing he would know about himself was that he would not feel *awkward* or *alone*. He opted out of treatment after three sessions.

Resistance to change grid   Sometimes it is useful to do a resistance-to-change grid in which, as with the implications grid, a person's constructs are compared with each other. Hinkle designed this grid also, and it was to test out his idea that laddered constructs are the more superordinate (important) ones. In addition, he showed that superordinate constructs have the most implications. It is because they have the most implications that they are the most resistant to change.

The questioning for the resistance-to-change grid goes along these lines: 'You say that you prefer to be a *gentle* rather than an *aggressive* person and *intelligent* rather than *stupid*; tomorrow morning when you wake up you will have changed EITHER from being a *gentle* person to being an *aggressive* person OR from being *intelligent* to being *stupid*. *Which would you find it easier to change on?*' When two superordinate constructs are paired in that way, there is a gut reaction. Both seem to be utterly impossible. The threat can be massive for you are asking the person to face up to the possibility of change in their core role construing. No one can face that lightly.

The easiest way to score this is to have a sheet of paper set out as overleaf

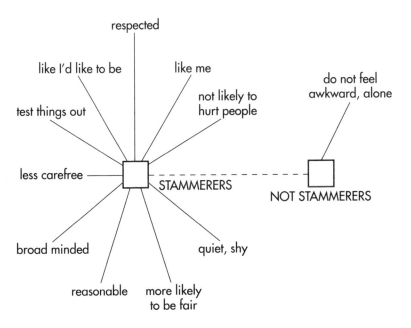

FIGURE 4.2 *Cluster from Amir's implication grid*

for eight constructs, and then simply to circle the construct in each pair on which the person says they will find it easier to change.

1–2	2–3	3–4	4–5	5–6	6–7	7–8
1–3	2–4	3–5	4–6	5–7	6–8	
1–4	2–5	3–6	4–7	5–8		
1–5	2–6	3–7	4–8			
1–6	2–7	3–8				
1–7	2–8					
1–8						

Grids are, for the most part, highly verbal in content. But there are other, less verbal ways of exploring a client's construing.

These Aids as Part of the Counselling Programme

Several instances have been mentioned in which it has been suggested that these aids in personal construct counselling aimed at helping the counsellor understand the client also help the client understand themselves.

It is often the case that the number of sessions has to be limited. This particularly applies to business or career-counselling settings. Mary was a financial manager in a large organisation. She had the impression that people did not think too highly of her as a person and one day had a stand-up row with a woman superior. She was sent on a management course. Mary, however, decided that she wanted to find out more about herself and the reasons for her outburst, her migraine headaches and her dissatisfaction with aspects of her personal life. On listening to her account of herself the counsellor and Mary agreed to make a contract for five sessions.

She first completed a self-characterisation. This led Mary to recognise how important it was for her to *have a sense of balance, an interest in people* together with a very great enjoyment of physical activities – which linked to a possible alternative of becoming a professional yacht-master.

In the third session Mary completed a ratings grid. This showed up clearly that her superior with whom she had had the row and 'others' wanted her to see her job as a 'people' job. This was what she felt strongly about but saw it as unrealistic as the job was so defined. The dilemma was uncovered. Using laddering once more and the ABC method of enquiry Mary was able to spell out more clearly for herself what alternatives were available to her. By the last session Mary felt she had enough insight into her problems to enable her to move forward.

Non-verbal Explorations of Construing

So far, most of the procedures discussed have been dependent on verbal exchange between counsellor and client. They might, in fact, be seen largely as structured conversations. Not all clients, however, can readily express their thoughts and feelings in words and other means of accessing their construing of things may be helpful to them.

Drawing   A young man was asked to write a self-characterisation. He found it impossible as he felt very confused at the time as to who he was. He came, instead, with a painting, which vividly showed a conflict between his heart and his mind and expressed the turmoil he felt through the flames which surrounded both areas and a thick black substance swirling underneath. Having painted the picture, he was more able to speak of it. Art therapists will be familiar with such a process (as mentioned in Chapter 2).

FIGURE 4.3 *Ill at ease*

Apart from encouraging such spontaneous expression, it is sometimes helpful to suggest that a person draw a situation – and its contrast. One example is given below, where a client first drew a situation in which she felt ill at ease. Figure 4.3 shows her sitting at a table with others and we can see how the figure representing herself is turning away almost in a frenzy. She elaborated on this, saying that it represented how she felt at the regular staff meetings which took place where she worked. She hated the formality of it, the way people seemed to relish attacking one another and dragging her in when she only wanted to run away. Even in so simple a drawing (and no artistic skill is needed), her frustration and panic are clear. Figure 4.4 shows her at home with just one other person. At peace, listening to music, with a cat on her lap.

These drawings summarised her difficulties very well. She enjoyed many aspects of her work as a teacher, but hated the 'politics' of it and any exposure in a group situation. She was very much happier with one other companion, feeling much more 'herself' at home than in public. We had much work to do to make things at work more tolerable, but using the first picture as a basis, reconstruction was set in train by her thinking of what changes she could make to the drawing to take some of the tension out of it. In another version of this picture, she moved the figure of

FIGURE 4.4 *At peace*

herself, so that she was sitting next to someone she felt more at ease with on the staff. This immediately made her feel less 'alienated'. Then she surprised me by adding some windows to the drawing, wide open, which certainly altered its claustrophobic atmosphere. She asked for the windows to be opened at the very next meeting and felt more in control when the others agreed.

As Ravenette (1999) has shown in his work with children, such paired drawings can also bring out aspects of a person's experience which are less available to them – the darker side of their feelings about themselves, perhaps. When asked to show how she felt now and how she wanted to be, a young woman drew a tightly shut flower first, then another whose petals were 'open to the sun'. But her anxiety about such a development was symbolised by her adding a threatening-looking bird hovering over the second flower. In their recent book *The Child Within* (1998) Butler and Green describe several ways of exploring a child's sense of themselves, including a useful way of establishing a child's 'self-image profile'. This is the first book to describe how personal construct psychology can be applied to understanding children with a wide range of problems in a wide range of situations.

Those working with children in particular will be familiar with the use of clay models to help a child express the relationships between people, for example by grouping them on the table as he or she sees them communicating with one another. And this kind of procedure can be helpful for adults too. Modelling in clay can convey intense feelings even more expressively than drawing. And in groupwork, elaborating a large painting together can show much of the way members are construing each other. There are, of course, numerous permutations on these few ideas.

Depending partly on the skills of the counsellor, music, movement and drama can also form an important part of the exploration of clients' construing. And these activities may form a valuable aspect of the process of change itself. We shall be looking at role play and enactment in Chapter 5.

Observation and inference   Finally, our attempt to 'read' each other in order to understand will always include our observation of facial expression, posture, bodily tension and relaxation and so on. In daily life this occurs often at a low level of awareness. We are picking up cues nevertheless. In counselling, sensitivity to such things is a crucial part of our interaction with clients. Often there is a telling contradiction between what the person is saying and the tone of voice, the expression on the face, the position of the body. A client may, at times, be unable to speak, but how they sit may tell us much. It is not for us to rush in immediately with 'interpretations'. But we might tentatively suggest what we think we observe, checking it out with the client. If this is not appropriate, we register some moment which seems to convey important information and see whether later movements, gestures, facial expressions confirm our impression. It is all part of our subsuming of the client's construing.

Some of the earliest signs of change, which is the subject of our next chapter, may come in this form, rather than in words. Loosening of a client's construing may show itself first in bodily relaxation. Sudden tightening under threat may be revealed perhaps only through clenching of the hands. Greater eye contact may show the development of more confidence in the counselling situation. Choosing to sit in another chair could be a significant experiment on the client's part. We have shown how one client was able to take active steps to ease a difficult situation after she had made changes to a drawing. And it will be seen that many of the ideas put forward in Chapter 5 involve the client in far more than talk. Words are, of course, important in most approaches to counselling but we lose much if they alone are relied upon.

SUMMARY

There are many methods and techniques that have come from personal construct psychology that can help define more clearly how a person is construing her world. The personal construct counsellor is not limited to these. He has all invented methods at his disposal and can even invent his own. All such methods are short cuts to get more quickly at what it is likely to be that is preventing the client dealing with her own life. The criterion for choice of method is that it should help the counsellor understand more about the client's world and, perhaps, help the client start the reconstruing process.

In the context of short-term counselling, the personal construct methods themselves can form the basis of the counselling programme itself as opposed to being solely instruments of enquiry.

Chapter 5 describes the counselling process as a process of reconstruction.

5

COUNSELLING AS A PROCESS
OF RECONSTRUCTION

It should be clear from our discussion of the processes involved in exploring the problems clients present and the contexts in which each person experiences those difficulties that 'reconstruction' does not begin only when 'exploration' ends.

The client often starts to look at life from a different perspective when completing procedures designed primarily to provide the counsellor with insights into her construing. Writing a self-characterisation which looks towards the future, or completing a grid, can bring the client that much nearer to coming to grips with important goals in life. As the counsellor listens and attempts to understand, the client may, perhaps for the first time, construe himself or herself as someone worth bothering about. And this would be a major reconstructive step.

Now we shall look specifically at the nature of the change process in counselling. As we stated at the start, counselling does not set out 'stages' through which the client moves, nor does it prescribe areas that must be explored – such as childhood events. It is the application of the theory and philosophy of the psychology of personal constructs to the formulation of the client's problem and then the identification of alternative ways of construing that may lead the client along the road of self-experimentation once more.

This rather abstract approach makes any description of it look rather technique bound, but this is not the case, as we hope will become apparent in our discussion of counselling with a specific client in Chapter 6. There is no rule-book. There is only a set of professional constructs (the set of goggles the counsellor wears) used to bring about desired changes in the clients' views of themselves and their worlds. We can therefore only provide examples of how a counsellor might make sense of specific problems being experienced by the client and what she might do to help the client move on.

We shall first look at some of the more superordinate constructs: ways of helping the client loosen and tighten their construing system; ways of bringing about change through reducing or increasing the meaning of certain constructs; the accessing of pre-verbal construing; and the replacing of ways of construing which are proving ineffective. Methods for reducing hostility and helping the client to deal with guilt will then be considered. The importance of the experimental approach, the testing out of predictions and consideration of outcomes is stressed throughout.

THE CREATIVE ASPECTS OF CHANGE

All change is an act of creation. Each one of us knows that when we decide to give up some piece of behaviour, we have created a new 'me'. Just so with counselling. There are many ways of helping a person change their construing of themselves and the world that mills around them, but we will stick to those that stem directly from Kelly's theory. For it is the theory that counts. It is the theory that guides the counsellor in the creative partnership with the client. To help the client reconstrue, the counsellor is free to use any technique with which he or she feels confident. This is important. It is the theory that is constant, not the techniques. Kelly spells it out like this:

> There is no . . . particular set of techniques of choice for the personal construct (therapist) counsellor. The relationship between (therapist) counsellor and client and the techniques they employ may be as varied as the whole human repertoire of relationships and techniques. It is the orchestration of techniques and the utilization of the on-going process of living and profiting from experience that makes (psychotherapy) counselling a contribution to human life. (Kelly, 1969c: 223)

Some examples follow of how one may help someone change their construing in relation to theoretical constructs.

TECHNIQUES FOR HELPING A PERSON TIGHTEN THEIR CONSTRUING

The construct *tight–loose* and how this relates to creativity was discussed quite fully in Chapter 3. There we gave examples of how two people were able to approach an aspect of life differently by either loosening or tightening their construing. Here we look at some of the ways that have been suggested for helping an individual change the *process* of their construing.

Tightening is one end of the creativity cycle. It is a way in which the client may elaborate her view of the world by becoming more explicit about it. Tightening involves imposing some orderliness on construing so that subordinate constructs are more neatly subsumed under superordinate ones. We are then able to judge our own behaviour.

Judging or Superordinating

One way to encourage tightening of construing is to ask the client to comment on his own statements. You may ask such questions as 'Exactly how does this compare in importance with what you said earlier about . . .?' Or 'You have told me a number of thoughts and feelings you have had, but I do not yet have a clear idea of how you see them all fitting together.' Those who favour tight ways of construing are often judgement oriented.

Summarising

In order to summarise something one has to place events in some kind of order – this is tightening. 'What do you see as the main things we have sorted through during our last three sessions?' 'We are coming to the end of our session now. It would be very helpful for me if you would summarise what we have covered as you see it.'

Kelly suggests that we might ask some clients to write a summary of each session when they get home and to bring this summary to the next session. It can be used as the basis of the session for those who find it difficult to express themselves. It can be read out, discussed and used to form the basis of new enquiry.

Summarising is also useful in the laddering process. As the client struggles to find the right words to express some very unclear superordinate and important idea, you can ask him to summarise what he has said or ask if there is one word or a short sentence that will sum it all up.

Historical Perspectives

Constructions can be tightened by asking the client to look at things historically: 'When did you first have these ideas?'; 'What does this remind you of?'; 'How did you come to think this way about the problem?'

Relating Ideas to Those of Others

A fourth way of tightening construing is to ask such questions as: 'Who are you most like?'; 'Do you know anyone else who thinks this way?' This, of course, is also often historical in content.

The Direct Approach

You might ask directly: 'I am not clear what you are telling me. Would you mind explaining it to me again, please?' If appropriate, you can go on and ask the person to *say it again*.

Challenging the Construction

A sixth method is to challenge directly what the client is saying. This has to be done with care as it may easily cause too much threat to the client. It can also invalidate the client's belief that she is wholly accepted by the counsellor. 'How do you reconcile what you are saying now with what you said last week about X?'

On occasion it may be useful to show your incredulity at what the client is saying. On one occasion, for instance, Luke (who stuttered) was desperately trying to work out why he preferred to have status rather than not. His ladder led him to focus on the possibility of being refused by someone and how he would not know what to do if this happened. The following eventually emerged and, while looking fairly tight in construction, was very tentative, as indicated by his questioning tone of voice at the end:

Luke: Well, I think that this is the thing. If one has status or is respected (which is the same thing), then if someone is infinitely respected then they would say what they want to a person, who would immediately rush off and do it. If a person commanded zero respect and they said to someone 'I want so and so' the reply would be 'Go and do it yourself.' Everybody lies somewhere between these two. But I suppose the majority of people would be happy about having people refuse to help them or having people downright rude to them.

My (Fay) response to this most extraordinary idea (to me at least) was: 'Oh, come off it. I am not!!' Luke came right back with: 'Well, you'd probably be able to sum up the situation and sort of say something to make them change their mind . . . Wouldn't you?'

It seemed important to invalidate this idea of his as soon as possible so I elaborated a partially true account of going into a garage and asking for some air in my car tyres. On having the machine pointed out to me with the implication that I should do it myself, I left 'because I did not know how to do it'. But I did not turn round and say 'I can't do it'. There was real incredulity in his voice as he said 'Why was that?' His amazement increased as he thought of my failure to deal with such a situation. We finished as follows:

> *Fay*: I don't think you can assume that everyone can deal with all situations automatically and that it is only you who can't. It is not necessarily anything to do with speech.
> *Luke*: That is a very interesting thing, because I feel that fluent speakers can deal with any situation and that if I was fluent I would be able to do so too.

Ask for Validating Evidence

'How do you know that?' 'What kind of evidence would it take to convince you that you were wrong?' I asked Trixibell, 'How will you know when you have as much love as you need?' She replied, 'I can never have enough!' Others often answer in terms of 'more than anyone ever needs'. Either way they are saying that there is no possibility of there ever being any validating evidence. This question serves to bring the person into contact with the reality (or fantasy) of their demands on life. No one in the whole wide world can validate their experiences. The world always fails these people. The questioning brings them face to face with their own hostility.

Word and Time Binding

A client may have a whole sea of confusion around some issue. It is something which he has great difficulty in pinning down. He needs to find the right word to express what is meant. 'Is that the right word or is it not? If not, why not?' 'What other word might we use?' When encapsulated by that word the construct will tend to become more impermeable – it will not so easily take in new elements. The counsellor needs to note such word binding so that the construct may be loosened again should occasion demand.

Personal construct counselling differs from the psychoanalytic approach in having no place for a specific construct of 'ego strength' and in not making a requirement of 'emotional insight'. Yet there is agreement that words usually play a major role in the process of reconstruction. Kelly suggests that what analysts call 'emotional' might better be understood as not being 'word bound'.

> The person who is anxious cannot completely verbalize his anxiety; if
> he could he would no longer be anxious. Of course, he can demonstrate
> his anxiety in part by means of words, sometimes a torrent of words.
> But the words are the loosely held elements in the seething pot of his
> anxiety. The word symbols which would give those elements structure
> and continuity are yet to be found. Indeed the structure and continuity
> must themselves first be found. (Kelly, 1955: 804; 1991: Vol. II, 173)

The following verbatim excerpt is taken from a session with Roland who is aware that some change has occurred but he cannot quite place what it is. This has pushed him into a position of extreme anxiety because he is unable to get a hold of what this all implies for him. He is reporting on a situation in which he found himself behaving and feeling in an unpredicted way.

> *Roland*: It was, it was very peculiar, I'm very confused about it, which is
> partly why I am being so hesitant um, um. The reason I'm
> confused was that it was all very eh, *unintense* um I was feeling a
> lot of the things I have felt in the past but at a very low level of
> intensity, um [*laughs*]
> *Fay*: Did that make you uneasy?
> *Roland*: I just felt, I just find it difficult to understand really.
> *Fay*: Could it not simply be that this is how change comes about that
> you are left almost with a habit – that the emotions are withdrawn
> from . . .
> *Roland*: Yeah, yes that was partly what it felt like except . . . yes, um I
> don't know, as I say I feel very confused about it um . . . um. Oh.
> *Fay*: Can you spell out the confusion for me?

Roland: Well I suppose the main, well . . . I wasn't very anxious. I mean
   anxious – I was more anxious than what I would like [*laughs*]
Fay: Was it a general apprehension rather than being uncomfortable?
Roland: It wasn't particularly uncomfortable, um, I mean, I had, it
   was . . . there was sort of columns, but, um, which is a peculiar
   way of describing it, but it felt like columns of, eh, of, oh, anxiety
   and I felt myself going red and I suppose if you like embarrassed
   several times. But it seems that if I'm actually prepared to relax
   and do things – see what happens, em . . . I'm more likely to find a
   sense of direction instead of lurching off in a panic.

With some struggling through the 'seething pot of his anxiety' we found
a hook to hold some of it down. It was to do with a sense of direction. He
had so far spent his life without direction, being unable and unwilling to
take on the role of adult. He was the man who saw himself as 'not yet successful'. He suddenly saw that he had moved on to such an extent that not
having a sense of direction was a problem. Mixed in with having a sense
of direction was massive threat – he was someone who could not contemplate failure and choosing a path to the future must mean you could
be wrong. But look at the opposite pole – 'lurching off in a panic'. No
wonder he feels trapped – locked into a way of construing that is untenable either way.

Roland: I do feel somewhat trapped. I feel I've got myself into a whole
   lot of circumstances which I've [*laugh*] sort of arrived at.

He's got somewhere and is not sure he wants to be there. He spells out
the advantages of the past position.

I only really want to see socially, um . . . people I know I am fond
of [*laugh*] . . . I am not very interested in getting to know new
people . . . partly what I want is that, eh, to be dependent on a
small group of people . . . em, so that I can be independent in
other ways . . . as a kind of base.

He now puts into words some of the advantages of staying as he is and the
role played by his symptom. It keeps him in his cosy home setting.
   His laughter plays an important part in this dialogue. With no words to
tie anything down, laughter can be used to ensure that anything said will
not be taken too seriously. He used it whenever he was pointing to the

conflict between his previous state and his perceived new one with an indication that his old state is the more desired one.

The personal construct counsellor has no problems about whether or not to accept the behaviour of a client whose only way of giving expression to his construing is to 'act it out'. The acting out of roles in dealing with personal relationships and the use of 'role play' within the counselling sessions go well together. Kelly points out that even at the end of counselling in which change has clearly been in the desired direction, the client may be able to talk *about* it, but not be able to say what it *was* that enabled him to move onwards. It is not fixed firmly by words.

Time binding is straightforward. It means dating a construct. The construct was applicable in childhood but is so no longer. Kelly gives the example of miracles as having been time bound for some. 'There used to be miracles but not any longer in the twentieth century.'

Hazards of Premature Tightening of Construing

Asking a client to tighten too soon can be counter-productive. The client needs to have experience with the newly formed constructions, to have elaborated them, to have seen that they stand up to the test of time. Premature tightening means there is not enough experiential evidence yet available on which to base a tightened construction. Someone who is building up a whole new world of being someone else – perhaps someone who is assertive rather than someone who is diffident – can be faced with catastrophic anxiety if tightened too fast. She is forced to look at the implications of what is going on. She sees that there really is very little to sustain her as an assertive person when compared with the very predictable world of being in the background and diffident. So she not unnaturally goes back to what she knows. She becomes diffident again. Alternatively she may come face to face with the fact that, in playing around with assertiveness, she is behaving in an aggressive – unacceptable – way. She faces the guilt of not only being unlike 'herself' but also being something she considers to be 'bad'.

TECHNIQUES FOR ENCOURAGING LOOSENING OF CONSTRUING

With loose construing order and judgement are at a minimum and experiencing is paramount. Loosened construing takes place at a lower level of cognitive awareness. Before embarking on loosening exercises, the counsellor will, of course, have made quite sure that the client's construing is not already so loose that she is in danger of making a current problem worse. With Roland, for example, one of the formulations was that on no account was there to be any attempt to loosen his construing further. But in very many cases loosening is essential so that the creativity cycle can get under way.

In helping a client loosen construing or in working with a client who is predominantly loose, the tempo of the interaction is considerably slowed down. Loose construing and quick repartee are unlikely to occur together.

There are four main ways in which a client may be helped to loosen aspects of their construing system: relaxation, chain association, recounting dreams and the counsellor's uncritical acceptance of the client.

Relaxation

It is virtually impossible to relax your body and keep your attention sharply focused on some issue or event. This is a good example of Kelly's insistence that we are best construed as a totally integrated person. There are many methods for helping a client relax. Psychoanalysts typically have the client lie on a couch but that is by no means essential. Deep relaxation can be accomplished very satisfactorily with the client in a comfortable chair. If your body loosens so will your constructions.

Chain Association

This is also a procedure used by the psychoanalysts; you ask the client to say whatever comes into her mind. To report *everything* that comes into the mind is, of course, preposterous. 'It is virtually impossible to keep one's tongue flapping in hot pursuit of all fleeting thoughts and images' (Kelly, 1955: 1034). The personal construct counsellor urges the client to 'give a running account' of what is going on without deliberately picking out those ideas or images that are more important than others.

There are a number of ways of dealing with clients' difficulties in producing loose constructions. First, the client may have difficulty getting started. He can be asked to just let his mind wander without saying anything for a while and then to review what he has been thinking about. Or the counsellor may choose the starting point, such as a relatively innocuous word, incomplete sentence or a picture. This can be extended, if she thinks there is pre-verbal material involved, by suggesting that the client *associates away from* the starting point. As all experienced counsellors know, it is difficult to move away from an important issue.

Second, the client may appear to be putting up a smokescreen of 'irrelevancies'; but with concentration on the part of the counsellor, these may begin to fall into some perceptible pattern. It is important to bear in mind that the client may be acting out some construing that is pre-verbal. In this case the counsellor has to pay attention to the *way* the client is behaving. These seeming irrelevancies may also be examined with an eye to their possible submerged poles. The question becomes: 'Now what, to this client's way of thinking, stands in contrast to what he is saying or doing?'

A third approach is to break up tight constructions. This is what the use of chain association and relaxation methods are really all about. The counsellor may have to make positive interventions by asking questions or commenting on the feeling component of construing. Trixibell's tight construing was broken up for a while in our first session when I asked her what she was *feeling* at that moment. Her feelings were allowed to come to the surface and she burst into tears. Chain association and relaxation methods are useful in highlighting the feeling component in the comparative safety of the consulting room. Questions may be: 'But what does all of this *feel* like to you? What is it reminiscent of?' 'What does all of this vaguely resemble?' 'Does it feel like something you have told or experienced before and yet cannot quite put your finger on?' 'You are telling me facts – let's not deal with facts just now, let's deal with deeper meanings, with pressures, with lurking anxieties, with vague uneasiness, with yearnings, with ideas that are hard to put into words.'

Sometimes loosening is achieved by asking the client not to say anything 'important'. In attempting to do this the client may bring into play his loose pre-verbal construings and possibly also reveal the contrast poles. All these may be heard by the counsellor with a well attuned ear.

Dreams

Dreams are loosened construing *par excellence*: not only loose but often pre-verbal as well. As dreams are told they often change in the telling – at the end the person feels that the beginning must have been different. This does not matter because in the first instance, the counsellor is concerned with how the client reports it rather than what was dreamed about.

Dreams come in all shapes and sizes. Kelly mentions a few types of dreams.

First, *mile-post dreams* are those great, vivid epics in which we feel we have been involved. Their vividness and the fact that they are so memorable suggest a certain degree of tightness. However, since they appeared in dream form there must be looseness somewhere. Kelly argues that the comprehensiveness and vividness suggest that there are superordinate constructions involved and that this indicates some underlying change taking place in the client's construing system. If this is so then counselling may be entering a new phase.

The counsellor should on no account attempt any interpretations of such dreams as the client will probably do his own interpretation when the time is ready for him to tighten. Kelly's (1955) example is of a young woman whose hostility, inability to show aggression and constriction had shown themselves in somatic symptoms such as anorexia and vomiting. She dreamed vividly of a meal she was preparing that her family liked. Her husband announced he was going off to the races. She threw the meal on the floor. She spontaneously interpreted the dream as a summary of her whole problem. Changes soon began to take place in her behaviour.

Kelly also identifies *pre-verbal dreams*, which are very vague, full of visual imagery and lack any personal interactions. Trixibell reported a dream in which she was a young child seemingly floating just off the ground and trying desperately to reach a figure that was visible through some sort of mist. But she felt she was unable to reach this figure however hard she tried. Through her tears she began to express her fury at that figure who made no attempt to respond to her need for comfort. She went on to relate this fury to her feelings towards her mother.

Sometimes the dreamer pictures herself at the opposite end of her construct network. Trixibell, so eager to be loving to all concerned, might well have dreamed of expressing her fury at her mother instead of experiencing it during a session with a counsellor. Either way, she was exploring the submerged end of her construing of herself as an all-embracing loving person. When this happens, the counsellor hypothesises that the client may be ready to explore this area further and so start to elaborate their construing. It is very important that the counsellor is aware of this possibility so that the client's experiments are not misconstrued.

Finally, *gift dreams* are brought to please the counsellor! The dreams start to follow the counsellor's perceived approach. If this happens it is reasonable to suppose that little movement is taking place and that some reformulation of the counselling strategy is required.

Helping the client elaborate the dream   There are all sorts of questions that can be put to help the client recall the dream: for example, 'Was it a happy dream or a bad one?'; 'Was it simple or complex?'; 'Were there many people?'; 'What other dream or experience have you had which seems something like this one?'; 'Was the dream in colour?' Quite often the dream will be experienced much more clearly later on in the interview. In 'Searching for the core' Leitner (1985) goes straight for the client's most superordinate area of construing. When the client has described the dream, Leitner asks, 'What is the most important thing about the dream for you?' And then, 'What is the opposite to this?' As with all other dream work, care needs to be taken that the client is not overwhelmed by this.

Interpretation of dreams   Interpretations, if used at all, should never come early on in the client's reporting of a dream, because they have a tightening effect resulting in the destruction of the benefits to be derived from the loosening. Personal construct counsellors only ever use interpretations of a client's construing if they think the client is thereby enabled to make use of that other way of looking at the event. The counsellor will never interpret from a position of 'knowing'.

Gestalt therapy has some very useful methods for studying dreams. All have a tightening effect but can nonetheless present the client with their *own* interpretation of what may have been going on. Of course, these things may not have been going on in the dream itself, but they can give the client new insights. One person had problems with her female role. She kept becoming very angry and frustrated with a wide range of events but found it impossible to pin-point precisely what it was that bugged her. At her second counselling session she reported a dream of going up a path leading to a very lovely cottage, everything seemed peaceful, the garden was a mass of beautiful flowers and well tended. Yet she felt not only very hostile towards it all but also anxious. Using the gestalt method, she was persuaded to represent the dream from the standpoint of each of the elements in it: that is, she recounted the dream 'as if' she were the house; 'I am that house. I am well built and secure; well looked after', and so on. The same with the garden. Eventually she came to the path. 'I am a path leading through this lovely garden to this well tended house *and I am constantly being trodden on*; no one ever pays any attention to me, they ignore the fact that I have absolutely no weeds and am made up of beautiful pieces of pink, grey and white granite', and so on. She laughed as she finished, having clearly identified what, for her, was the problem.

This method of tightening up on the dream can be most illuminating but has to be handled with care. You are asking the person to tighten in areas which may lead anywhere. Of particular importance is the order in which the items are enacted. The counsellor can usually see where the main issue is likely to lie and is wise to leave this to the last.

Producing Loosening by Uncritical Acceptance

Uncritical acceptance is a general characteristic of the counsellor's role. However, it does also have other implications. Here it means not only passively accepting the client's world view, but also being careful not to question the loose constructions too closely even if understanding is minimal. Saying such things as 'I think I know how you feel' provides validation for the client's attempts at loosening constructions.

Hazards in Producing Loosened Construing

It is a good rule of thumb for a personal construct counsellor to believe that loosening for a client can be a real hazard. One must therefore have a reasonably clear idea of whether the client will be able to cope with the loss of control implicit in all loosening exercises before embarking on relaxation and so forth.

A client may sometimes appear to 'resist' attempts to persuade her to loosen her construing. Such resistance is always viewed as valid. It means that the counsellor has not got a clear enough view of what the client is being asked to do. There is a failure of communication between the client and counsellor. There may be too much threat. The client may be having too great a struggle to keep anchors firmly embedded in reality readily to countenance loosening their hold.

All sorts of things can happen if you attempt to help a client loosen her construing prematurely. Sometimes the counsellor may think he has encountered resistance to his loosening efforts when, in fact, the client is way ahead of him. The client may well be into the creativity cycle (loose to tight to loose construing and so on) and be dealing with some new ideas which do not have adequate verbal labels. All the client can do is to use selected elements that are making up this new construction. This can sound very concrete. As Kelly says: 'Another way of indicating the same thing is to say that an idea is likely to take shape before a suitable symbol is chosen to represent it; it is born before it is named' (Kelly, 1955: 1051; 1991: Vol. II, 344).

Counsellors can be the cause of resistance to loosening in clients by their too ready interpretations. This may threaten the client or simply divert him from the task – but either way the result is to tighten. The counsellor himself may come to be construed as a threatening person. If this happens, the counsellor must produce evidence to invalidate the construction. He has to make sure the client construes him as someone who will not jump down upon him the minute he has speculated on some matter, or take advantage of slips of the tongue. 'Stated in other words, the client may need to feel that his loose thinking will be accepted rather than challenged or put to the test' (Kelly, 1955: 1057; 1991: Vol. II, 348).

Whatever the cause of the resistance to loosening, and assuming the counsellor feels it right to persist, there are some methods, such as enactment, that she can use. For instance, many clients are able to enact themselves in a different role if it is presented 'as if'. A person may have doubts about their sex role and find it impossible to loosen up and talk about it. But that same person may be quite willing to enact the part of a person who has sex-role difficulties. Alternatively, this same person may be able to think loosely about art or the nature of the universe. While loosely thinking about art, the counsellor may be able to shift the context so that it becomes possible to think about sex roles in relation to art.

Signs of Impending Loosening

There are signs for which to be on the look out that will tell the counsellor that her goal of producing loosened construing in her client is about to be attained. The client becomes more difficult to follow. The voice pitch may drop; flow of speech slows, becomes less rhythmic with less emphasis on communication and more on thought production. The client looks less intently at the counsellor and is more likely to gaze into space; responds less quickly and seems less aware of the relevance of his utterances.

Difficulties in Loosening Construing

Of all our efforts to help someone change their ways of interpreting themselves and the world, attempts to bring about loosening are the most useful and the most hazardous. By its very nature, loosening is about giving up control, about giving up our ability to test out, to predict events. It is ventured upon only when the counsellor has made a clear diagnosis of what may be preventing the client from moving on and where the stumbling blocks may lie.

These hazards have already been touched on in our discussion of resistance. The client who is maintaining his grasp on the world by holding his construing under a tight rein can easily be faced with a world of chaos with an over-zealous counsellor bent on loosening at all costs. Kelly describes the effects in relation to psychotherapy but it is equally applicable to counselling:

> A zealous therapist who insists that the client release his tight grip upon precarious fragments of reality may, thereby, inadvertently plunge his client into a state of anxiety so severe as to require immediate institutionalisation.
>
> Psychotherapeutic loosening is indeed one of the most important procedures in the psychotherapist's armamentarium. Since it is a feature of creative thinking it may be skillfully employed in the more creative approaches to psychotherapy. But not all therapists are able to follow the procedure skillfully. It requires comprehensiveness and flexibility in one's own view-point to follow in hot pursuit, day after day, the twistings and turnings of another person's vagaries. Add to these difficulties the exasperating 'resistances' of clients who cannot manage this state of creative thinking, and add also the hazards of having a client who cannot progress out of it. This is the problem of psychotherapeutic loosening. (Kelly, 1955: 1060)

So much for the hazards implicated in premature loosening for the person currently finding the 'tight' mode most useful. But there are also hazards for the person who finds loose construing a successful way of warding off anxiety. Within reason, predictions can be variable, as long as there is some semblance of order. If one can make no prediction at all, then that is anxiety. Loosening can be a way of avoiding anxiety. If we keep our construing loose, so that our predictions are of the sort 'I expect him to behave in a kind way towards me, but I shall not be too surprised if I am wrong and he ignores me', we are unlikely to be invalidated. That also means we are unlikely to change. In its extreme form, this is the type of construing found in the thought disorder of schizophrenics (Bannister, 1962).

Ronald was someone who found comfort in loosened construing. This was to such an extent that one of the main counselling aims was to ensure that he was never given any encouragement to loosen further. He was already cut off from reality enough and it was a central concern not to precipitate him once again into that unreal world we call schizophrenia.

Moving To and Fro Between Tightening and Loosening

Counselling is not just concerned with *either* tightening *or* loosening, but with creativity – the movement from one to the other. In the early stages of counselling, loosening or tightening may take place over several sessions before a change is made to the other mode. However, it is always important to bring about some tightening during the last ten minutes of a session so that the client does not have to deal with the harsh realities of the outside world in too loose a state. In general, the counselling programme may involve several loosening sessions followed by several tightening ones. 'The therapist teaches the client how to be creative in reconstruing life' (Kelly, 1955: 1085; 1991: Vol. II, 367). As sessions progress, however, the cycle will become shorter until it may be that a whole cycle between tight–loose–tight or vice versa takes place in one session.

Kelly points out that it is a common error of inexperienced counsellors to try to alternate too rapidly. Taking your time is a common theme with counselling. No step must be taken in the counselling programme without some clear idea of what the client is being asked to do *in the client's terms*.

SOME OTHER CHANGES IN CONSTRUING

Tightening and loosening as a cyclical process may be at the core of reconstruction, but many other types of change are important.

Slot Change

Slot change occurs when it is agreed that it would be useful for the client to move themselves to the other pole of one of their constructs. If, for example, they see themselves as essentially 'unassertive', while others are regarded as 'assertive', it could be an enlightening experience to see what it feels like to behave assertively, first in the session with the counsellor, then in some carefully planned situation outside. Unless this other pole comes to have real meaning for the client which is compatible with the rest of the self-image, the change is not likely to be lasting. On the other hand, the experiment could lead to elaboration of some kind of alternative to lack of assertion which *is* found to be acceptable.

Using Existing Constructs in a New Situation

The second possibility is for the client to select a construct being used in one context and apply it to a new situation. An example of this came with a woman who wanted to return to work but had grave doubts about being able to be 'organised enough' to cope in an office. When we looked at the organisational gifts she had applied to bringing up a family, however, and the masterly planning involved in getting three children to three different schools, entertaining her husband's business friends at short notice and managing to attend some evening classes herself, her courage rose.

Accessing Pre-verbal Constructs

The notion of pre-verbal construing is so important that you will have found that it crops up in nearly every chapter. Helping the client to bring to awareness constructs which are for the moment inaccessible to them is central to therapy and some counselling and is likely to involve a long-term commitment. The counsellor may feel that a person's difficulty in a particular relationship, for example, is due to constructs formed very early on in life.

Bridget was continually disappointed in friends and lovers alike. They took her for granted, disregarded her needs, were selfish and uncaring. Although in the early sessions she spoke of her father with great affection and admiration and could only remember the fun she had with him before he died when she was 10, she gradually recalled times when he had 'let her down': the Sports Day when he didn't turn up; the first time she brought a friend home from school and he wasn't there. He forgot her birthday once and when she told him how upset she was he dismissed her as 'whining'. Bridget had 'buried' all these hurtful memories because she wanted to keep her romantic picture of her dead father. It all seemed to make sense, though, of her unsatisfied hunger for attention and signs of affection.

Testing the System for Internal Consistency

This is essentially a process of exploring aspects of a person's construing which appear to hold some confusion. In Chapter 4 (p. 65) we gave an illustration of how implicative dilemmas may be clarified, using Tschudi's ABC model. Where an important construct shows advantages and disadvantages to both poles, the client either cannot win or cannot move. Laddering may also reveal some kind of inconsistency. For example, a client who longed to be confident as opposed to lacking in confidence found, when we laddered the construct for more superordinate implications, he did not like what he found on the *confident* side. There were hints of *riding rough-shod over others*. In this instance, the man was able to challenge his former valuation of confidence above all things without difficulty. In others, such long-held beliefs may have to be reconstrued more gradually, often entailing a fresh look at how things currently are.

Testing Constructs for their Predictive Validity

Many of our constructs about people and, in particular, types of people, are formed very early on in life and never challenged. This can not only cause trouble but set a limit to possible relationship. A most obvious example comes with racial prejudice. A person may expect all people from a certain race to be the 'dirty, lazy, good-for-nothings' they had heard of when they were young, and may never test this theory out. Someone may have met one teacher who was 'authoritarian' and spend the rest of their lives assuming that everyone in a similar role will be the same. Expectations of ourselves may have a similar effect: a person who saw herself as not very bright when young may continue to have this self-construct, despite the evidence of much achievement. It is constructs such as these that the counsellor may be particularly concerned to have the client challenge and test out.

Increasing the Range of Convenience of Constructs

A client may have some useful constructs which they apply effectively in narrow contexts only, thus limiting possibilities. This was the transitive diagnosis with Ron. Ron felt that he could only be effective when engaged in work. There, though it exhausted him, he was absorbed, interested, 'alive'. He could watch things take shape and grow. He felt bad that he was restless and ill at ease at home with his family. He particularly regretted not being able to enjoy his young children's company. We clarified the differences between the two situations. Far from being absorbed in his children, he paid them very little attention. It had not even occurred to him that what they did or said could be of interest and his feeling of not being alive seemed to spring from the lack of these two aspects found in his approach to work.

It was suggested that he spend some time with his children and attempt to absorb himself in their play and see what there was of interest going on. The most striking result of his experiment was his realisation that 'things were taking shape' for them so clearly as they played and when he repeated the event he was aware of quite tangible growth in their understanding from day to day. Although he could not pretend that everything else was worth his involvement, many other activities began to be included in those constructs hitherto reserved for work. He came to counselling complaining of stress at work and the counsellor's initial prediction that dispersing some of his intense concentration on his job would ease things proved valid.

Decreasing the Range of Convenience of Constructs

Just as applying an important construct too narrowly can be limiting, so can applying it too comprehensively. For Luke, the range of convenience of the construct *has status – has no status* included almost everything – even Rowntree's fruit pastilles. Everything had a status value and it was important to have status. If there was any doubt about this he would stutter. By looking at the evidence he gradually came to the conclusion that, although it was still very important for *him* to have status, it was not really necessary to apply the construct *has status – has no status* to things like Rowntree's fruit pastilles.

Altering the Meaning of Constructs

We have said a number of times that it is not for counsellors to impose their constructions on their clients. Thus, any attempts to change the meanings a client imposes on events should be designed to free her from construing which is immobilising her in some way and have little to do with the counsellor's views of what is right or wrong. A young woman, for example, divided people into those who were 'charismatic' and those who were 'dull'. Not having what, in her eyes, it took to be charismatic, she had resigned herself to being dull and took little trouble to be otherwise. She assumed everyone else felt the same about her. It was all very depressing. She was asked to try on 'interesting' for size as the contrast to dull. It had little meaning for her in the abstract but as she elaborated it in terms of the way she might dress, the way she could talk and listen, the things she did and could do in the future, it all became more viable. She experimented with a number of largely behavioural changes and, above all, reconstrued the feedback she had always had from others. The meaning of 'dull' had inevitably changed in the process. She now saw it as implying 'not making the most of yourself'.

Creating New Constructs

Kelly regards this process as the most difficult and ambitious of all. Why should we do it and, if we must, how do we do it? One obvious need for new construing comes with encountering new experiences. Transferring to an entirely different culture can be a traumatic experience if we rely only on comparisons between it and our old setting. We need to construe new customs and attitudes by getting closely in touch with them ourselves so that out of the new experiences will come new constructions to help us predict our altered world better.

As we grow up and develop, the need for new constructions is ever present, although it is possible to 'make do' with old ones. We may approach school, adolescence, marriage, parenthood, loss and death with constructs taken on from others without challenge. If we do this we may fail to be fully involved in such experiences. In our last chapter we shall look at what is described as *the full cycle of experience* again and see that continual renewing of constructs is implied in personal construct psychology.

Difficulties in the Reconstructive Process

It is not easy to reconstrue and it is sometimes not possible to make the kinds of changes described in our earlier sections. Resistance to change is frequently met within counselling and, as we have said, its causes are to be found in the constructs of transition themselves. Anxiety will very often hold a client back, at least for a while, or threat may make the task seem too formidable. Guilt, the sense of dislodgement from the self you thought you were, can make any of us, for a while at least, hold back from facing further changes in our construing. But it is hostility which so often proves the greatest stumbling block. Much time and care may need to be spent in helping the client to overcome it.

METHODS FOR REDUCING HOSTILITY

The hostile client presents the counsellor with many difficulties. She has come for appeasement for her distress rather than a solution to it. The counsellor who challenges rather than appeases may have to face expressions of disappointment, or incompetence. The hostile client has already faced failure with her social experiments and so is not going to get burned again. She therefore behaves in a way that 'proves' she was right all along. The counsellor will face difficulties in producing any movement.

As a first step, one way to start trying to break the hostility knot is to try to reduce the feelings of chaos that threaten unless it is maintained. Susan was encouraged to look at areas in life that were her own and over which she had control. There was listening to music; her stamp collection; and a couple of friends. In this way the hostility was given some boundaries. The price the counsellor has to pay for this exploratory, aggressive (Kellyan) behaviour of the client is to accept additional evidence of hostile construing for the time being.

With some predictive structure established, it may now be possible as a second step to introduce opportunities for further aggressive explorations. The counsellor can emphasise that he is there to support the client in every way possible and that she can therefore rely on him while she gently experiments with people's reactions in various ways. For instance, Susan was encouraged to express her feelings about her mother in the way she talked about her. In responding to this it was important that the counsellor did not appear to appease or share Susan's feelings about mother as that would make the exercise unproductive.

Helping a hostile client move forward – that is, to be prepared to stop making sure that things worked out the way they predicted rather than accept that they are wrong and actively explore alternatives – can be a long and difficult task. The client often tires before any perceptible results have been achieved. With Susan, it took many sessions before she was even able to let feeling enter her voice as she talked about mother. Hostility has a powerful immobilising effect on us all.

Hazards in Reducing Hostility

Hazards of helping the hostile client explore alternatives aggressively are numerous. If the client becomes too active in her aggressive explorations, she may experience guilt – 'By behaving in this way I am becoming a bad daughter.' She will then protect herself by constricting her world back to where it was before. If the client comes to see the extent of her own hostility before she has a workable alternative outlook on life, 'the therapist . . . may wake up some morning to find that his prize therapy case has ended up in suicide or a psychotic break' (Kelly, 1955: 891; 1991:

Vol. II, 234). Another hazard is the effect of aggressive behaviour on this previously hostile person's part on her family and close associates. People actively elaborating their worlds can often be very threatening to others.

TRANSFERENCE PROCESSES IN COUNSELLING

In Chapter 2 we referred to some of the possible expectations which Kelly suggests the client may have of counselling. He also invites us to ask ourselves 'In what role is the client now casting me?' – a question he believes we should continually keep in mind. He lists the kinds of roles the client may set up initially: parent, protector, absolver of guilt, authority figure, prestige figure, ideal companion and so on. As always, however, his emphasis is on change, and while transference and countertransference do not hold such a central position in personal construct counselling as in more analytic approaches, the need to construe changes here is obviously of considerable importance and may loom large in work with some clients.

In 'secondary transference', where the client applies 'a varying sequence of constructs from figures of his past', the counsellor is seen as incidental to the client's perceptions, with the constructions placed upon him or her lifted directly from former experiences. Constructs are 'tried on for size' and their validation or invalidation by the counsellor will have significance for the way in which the client will approach not only the counsellor but others in his life. Such transferences can be used 'as a basis for reorienting the client's constructions of other persons'. The counsellor can play varying parts and thus enable the client to develop a versatile capacity for role relationships with different kinds of people.

With 'primary transference', however, the counsellor, far from being incidental to the process, is pre-empted into a single role by the client, which becomes highly elaborated and allows for no such variety. The client becomes attached in a very dependent way and it is extremely difficult to resolve the relationship. Though undoubtedly coming from the past, constructs are applied to the counsellor in an unvarying way and elaborated in an organised fashion with respect to many aspects of the counsellor's behaviour, assumed interests, daily life and so on – until the counsellor seems to be 'the latent topic of the interview and the client is no longer concerned with himself'. Far from being a useful phenomenon, Kelly sees such a development as unproductive and an obstacle to movement and change on the part of the client.

It is important, therefore, for the counsellor to be alert to the potential development of such dependency. It is even more vital to be aware of any counter dependency transference, with the counsellor projecting his or her own needs on to the client. Here client and counsellor may become stuck in a 'me and thee' situation which leads nowhere in terms of the client's life outside. Where there is such primary transference Kelly warns against too much loosening of construction, particularly before any break in the sessions. He suggests that the counsellor 'seek always to maximise the client's own external resources as an ultimate protection against collapse during the course of reconstruction'. In addition, the use of 'free roles and counter roles' is advocated. Here the counsellor plays the part of the client's mother, father, boss, teacher rather than being himself. Then, in role reversal, the client takes on these parts. Through these procedures the client elaborates his relationships with others, rather than building up his image of the counsellor and his relationship with him or her.

Kelly notes that the transference of constructions on to the counsellor appears to go in cycles. The client never lays everything out at once but seems to test out certain role constructs, become more dependent for a while, then, on completion of each major reconstruction of an area, transferences on to the counsellor may become quite superficial again and dependency is reduced. This is seen as marking the end of a *transference cycle*. Awareness of these processes would seem to be important when considering discontinuing the counselling series. The end of a cycle would be appropriate for a break or termination, depending on whether a new cycle was needed to encourage further change within the counselling partnership.

ENACTMENT

Kelly uses the term 'enactment' rather than 'role playing' when discussing the use of the technique in counselling because of his very specific use of the term 'role' in another context. In his discussion of the sociality corollary he speaks of 'role' as 'a psychological process based upon the role player's construction of aspects of the construction systems of those with whom he attempts to join in a social enterprise' or 'an ongoing pattern of behaviour that follows from a person's understanding of how others who are associated with him think'. His classification of different kinds of therapeutic enactment is very comprehensive but he places most emphasis, as we shall here, on 'casual' enactment procedures in individual counselling. Here the parts can be structured with client and counsellor agreeing in advance as to how the parts are to be played out, or the enactment may develop more spontaneously out of something which is being discussed.

The function of enactment procedures is to help clients to elaborate aspects of their construing, to provide the means for experimentation within the safety of the counselling situation, to protect them from tackling more threatening issues outside before they are ready, and to enable them to see themselves and their problems in another perspective. Kelly sees the procedures as particularly useful in clarifying the client's approach to situations which they have so far only described. Through the scenes set up between them, client and counsellor can become aware of aspects of the client's behaviour and feelings which he or she may have found hard to put into words. The counsellor may also draw attention to important issues for other people in their lives of which the client had not been aware.

One very important feature of Kelly's approach to enactment is his use of the exchange of parts. In the first version, perhaps, the client is him or herself and the counsellor plays someone with whom there is difficulty. They then exchange, with the counsellor depicting the client and the latter the other person. Much can come of this. First, it enables the counsellor to stand more surely in the client's shoes and to understand more fully how he or she feels. Second, it gives the client the opportunity to catch something of the position and experience of the person with whom they are in difficulty.

Andrew saw himself very much as the victim of his parents' handling of him as a child. Throughout a long counselling series he had complained of his father's indifference and his mother's criticism and self-pity. He announced that he intended to tell her 'once and for all' when they met the next day what he thought of her and what she had done to him. It was proposed that we should enact that meeting. First, Andrew was himself. I (Peggy in this instance) was the recipient of years of pent-up anger. As his mother I was made to feel guilty and destructive. But I also told him something of my own pain in relation not only to him but his unresponsive father, who was now dead. This in itself was something Andrew had not considered and he was very thoughtful when the 'scene' ended. Then we reversed roles. I stuck to his script but he presented her as even more defensive to begin with and then had her turn on him with anger for *his* self-pity and lack of concern for anyone else. The dialogue lasted less than ten minutes. The effect was profound.

For the first time Andrew had attempted to see things through his mother's eyes. He still felt fairly justified in what he said to her but recognised that she too might have had a good deal to be depressed and angry about. In a hostile attempt to cancel out some of his painful understanding he asked whether I had been talking to his mother and had 'planned it all'. I won't say that thereafter all was well between them but from then on Andrew focused a good deal more on what he could do about himself and very little on the iniquities of his parents.

In other instances, a client may want to experiment with new ways of dealing with certain people or situations in life – being more assertive, perhaps, showing more friendliness or dealing with a new experience with less anxiety. Enacting what is to come may be very useful preparation. To begin with, showing more assertion may come out as the client's contrast pole of 'being aggressive' but enactment allows for experimentation with a number of alternatives to this. Indications of friendliness may be foreign to the client and the counsellor's show of interest in someone, for example, may give a lead. Approaching a new experience with a view to finding out what is entailed may be demonstrated as more effective than plunging in or running away because of anxiety.

Experiments With Living

As we have said, one of the strongest emphases in the approach to change is the attitude of experimentation. And there are a number of ways, besides enactment, in which this approach can be facilitated. If a client is dissatisfied with an aspect of life or the way they are, one obvious approach to changing things is to begin, in various ways, to elaborate how things *could* be. This can be done through conversation, through writing, drawing, modelling, dramatisation – any way, in fact, which dilates and/or loosens the client's construing. Once a picture has been formed of how things might be different, then the means for bringing change about can be evolved. And the only way to test out this experimental design is to put it, or some aspect of it, into action in life itself.

This can take many forms, from the simple step of taking up some new interest or course of study to a comprehensive reshaping of relationships. An example of the latter came with a man who had a communication problem and had missed out on many of the necessary experiences which teach us how to be a friend. After some preparation he set about developing the observations, behaviours and skills we had experimented with in the sessions. It was a long process and one which had some set-backs and disappointments. But it resulted in his learning a great deal more about other people that he had understood before and uncovering aspects of himself which he did not know were there. It went much further than any 'social-skills training' as it involved real changes in his total construing of relationship, rather than changes in behaviour only. Above all he learned to put himself in other people's shoes and accept their views as valid for them, even where he could not share them.

Other experiments aimed at changing a person's way of life may involve taking on new commitments, a new work role perhaps. This too may entail considerable threat and anxiety and should be prepared for with care. Any prospective new role should either be compatible with how the person construes themselves now or developed in the direction of the person's evolving constructions of themselves. And these will need to have been thoroughly explored and clear to both client and counsellor. Although people are encouraged to be adventurous, they are not urged to face massive anxiety by entering into an experience for which they have no constructions at all.

Sometimes a person comes for counselling through experience of loss. Someone close to them has died or left them. Part of their life has been taken away through loss of job or illness. They may indeed feel that they have come to a halt in terms of living. Here help is needed so that they may live effectively in a different way from before – without their spouse, without work, even without some physical or mental ability. It will need time and courage to evolve a new and 'whole' self in such circumstances. And still the foundation of what is accomplished will be the experiments that are planned in sessions and carried out in life itself. (See Neimeyer (1998) for more details of a personal construct approach to understanding grief.)

FIXED-ROLE THERAPY

Kelly described one specific method for aiding the reconstructive process, that of fixed-role therapy. He had been considerably influenced by Moreno's sociodrama in the 1930s and his development of enactment and fixed-role therapy can be seen as coming directly from this. It is important to note that Kelly described fixed-role therapy to show what the principles of his theory looked like in action. He was not presenting it as THE *METHOD*. Within his description of fixed-role therapy he also implicitly shows how the person may be seen as creating and recreating themselves.

It is perhaps the most comprehensive experiment client and counsellor develop together. Kelly describes it in great detail in Volume 1 of his original work and his ideas have been modified by Epting (e.g. 1984) and others. Its aim is to enable the client to experience change, try out new behaviours, new ways of looking at things, for a limited time and with the protection of the counsellor's support and the 'mask of make-believe'. It allows the client to learn the art of being different, without committing him or her to anything permanent.

The Fixed-role Sketch

The first step in preparing for a fixed role is the writing of a character sketch, based on the client's self-characterisation. The person depicted should not be totally alien to the client concerned, nor should he or she be some kind of ideal figure. The two sketches should have enough in common for the client to portray the new character comfortably, yet imply differences in outlook and behaviour which might usefully be experienced. Certain of the client's core constructs should be retained and themes introduced that he or she would find of value. It is essential that the client should feel that it is a character whom it would be good to know. The experiment should have real meaning and be acceptable to the client as a means of helping them move on in their own development.

Veronica came for counselling because at the age of 28 she suddenly woke up to the fact that she had no friends and felt that she could only look forward to 'a very lonely old age'. Her initial self-characterisation ran as follows:

Veronica is shy, highly strung and surrounds herself with a thick wall of reserve. Because of this she prefers a large circle of acquaintances rather than particular close friends.

She has a deep distrust of people and prefers either her own company or that of animals. Her favourite kind of holiday is one where she can be alone, buried in the countryside far away from the rat race.

She is quiet, but rarely bad-tempered, except in the mornings when she is like a completely different person. She has a quick defence mechanism, which results in her being snappy and having a sharp tongue occasionally.

She is a good listener, but can be too frank sometimes. However, she is loyal, honest and hard-working, taking a pride in her work.

She can be stubborn when she can manage to make up her mind. But can often see the other person's point of view which makes decisions hard sometimes. Her attitude to life is to do whatever you want to as long as it doesn't harm anyone else and to take people and things as you find them and not to prejudge and not to be too bothered about what other people think and do.

We – Veronica and I – worked for about six months on various aspects of her construing – she made considerable headway in challenging the mistrust of others she speaks of. It stemmed from her discovery at the age of seven that she had been adopted by her doting parents. Although she never doubted their love for her she had never forgiven them for 'deceiving' her. She came to see them as having made a misjudgement in deciding not to tell her, rather than being deceitful, and this change seemed to enable her to be less critical of others in her life too. We discovered that her bad temper in the mornings, which often set the tone for a really 'bad day', was the result of nightmares, which until she came for counselling she had only vaguely remembered. We spent some time exploring these dreams, which seemed to contain a good deal of unexpressed feeling from the previous day. As she gradually made sense of them and was more able to experience her negative feelings at the time, they decreased and her mood in the mornings improved.

She had to reconsider how good a listener she was, as it emerged that, while she listened, she was often feeling very critical of the views expressed and was, in fact, 'prejudging' others to a great extent. She had been far from taking people and things as she found them and her moves in this direction had already made relations with people at work much easier. Although all this had entailed a good deal of change in her life and shown her to be willing to be experimental, something more comprehensive seemed to be called for. She was given something to read on fixed-role therapy and she expressed herself willing to undertake it. With her own revisions, the following sketch was used as a basis for the character she was to portray over a period of two weeks. We spent some time choosing a name which she felt gave her the key to this other person:

Jennifer is a quiet but friendly person who has a large circle of acquaintances and one or two close friends who are very important to her. If she has any doubts about something they do or say, she is not afraid to speak out and clear the air. They are the sort of people she can contact any time but they will respect her need sometimes to be by herself. She is always very interested in what they are doing and how they feel about things.

She enjoys her work and does it well and conscientiously but she has come more recently to put as much into leisure activities, such as bird-watching and tennis. She is not particularly good at tennis, but, to her surprise, she enjoys it for its own sake and doesn't mind losing.

She shares her love of animals with her parents and is planning with their help to take the plunge soon and train to work with them as a full-time job. This will entail some risk and the loss of the security of her present job, but it should open new doors for her, which she longs for.

Jennifer is not pretty but her bright clothes and lively manner make her an attractive person to be with.

Veronica added the last sentence herself as she felt she needed some tangible change to what she considered her 'dowdy' appearance to help her to step into the new role.

The main elements of the sketch which we hoped would be useful were the greater involvement in leisure activities, which she set up before the experiment started, her developing more interest in the few closer friends she had already made and the elaboration of a possible future working with animals. She took two weeks of her holiday to pursue all this, reporting back four times in all during that time.

She made good headway in planning for training, presenting herself as 'Jennifer' to a number of prospective employers with a good deal more enthusiasm than she felt 'Veronica' would trust herself to show. The bird-watching she found highly enjoyable and although after the two weeks she never wanted to see another tennis racquet again, she learned a good deal from behaving 'as if' she didn't mind losing! Perhaps the greatest revelation to her was how hard it was to pay more attention to what others were thinking and feeling. She realised how often she cut them off to give her opinions or tell her story.

When the experiment was over, Veronica described it as 'very hard work', but she was glad she had done it. She was determined to carry through the project about changing her job and her parents were more than willing to back her. Although during the first week she had been rather disheartened by her lack of attention to others, this had improved and she decided that it was something she wanted to develop further. The change in clothes, which had been her idea, she decided to keep – in part. She would dress as Jennifer when she was feeling good or wanted to lift her spirits. She would sink back into her less interesting clothes when she just wanted to be comfortable.

Soon after this, we agreed that the counselling series should end, feeling that her life was on the move. She got in touch from time to time and in one letter she said that if she was feeling mistrustful of someone in a particular situation she asked herself, 'How would Jennifer deal with this?'

SUMMARY

In this chapter we have attempted to describe in detail some of the ways in which change or reconstruction may be brought about through personal construct counselling. We have focused on methods for changing the *processes* involved in clients' construing of themselves and their worlds in the light of our understanding of how they are approaching life when they come for help. It should be clear that this is not just a matter of changing a person's way of *thinking* about things. With our emphasis on the importance of the constructs of transition – anxiety, threat, guilt, hostility – the intense feelings involved at all levels of awareness are constantly borne in mind as part of the client's changing experience. And it is in action, in the person's experiments with ways of *behaving* differently that new constructions of events are tried and tested.

In our next chapter we shall draw together some of the ideas discussed so far in a description of counselling with one individual.

6

THE PROCESS OF CHANGE FOR LISA

INTRODUCTION

It will be clear that no one example of the counselling process can exemplify all the many issues of theory and practice discussed, but we hope to show how a client and counsellor worked together through exploration of the client's situation, clarification of her view of things (at different levels of awareness), early experimentation, review and plans for further action. The importance of personal construct psychology's theoretical framework, which governed the choice of specific interventions, will be stressed. (As in earlier chapters the 'I' refers to the author who was in the role of counsellor – in this particular case, Peggy.)

MEETING LISA FOR THE FIRST TIME

Reasons for Self-referral

Lisa telephoned to make an appointment, saying that she had heard about personal construct counselling from a friend who had attended some lectures I gave. She felt that she had 'come to a halt' lately and the approach sounded like the sort of help she was looking for. Knowing the student she referred to slightly, I imagined that she had given Lisa a fair account of Kelly's orientation, so Lisa would at least have some idea of what might be involved for her. (What I did not yet know, of course, was how she had construed what she heard in terms of her own needs.) We fixed a time for early the following week on the understanding that it was an opportunity for her to see whether she felt comfortable with me and would like to embark on a counselling series. I made a mental note to reassure her that there would be no communication between myself and the student if her friend had not already done so.

Observations

When she arrived, just two minutes late, she apologised for keeping me waiting and seemed uncertain whether to sit down before me when I invited her to. She was small, very pleasant looking and neatly dressed. She spoke quietly and hesitantly at first and blushed quite often as she told her story. It was obviously hard for her to look at me, although every now and then she glanced up to see my reaction to something she had said. Being concerned only to accept what she had to say uncritically and to try to understand the meaning of things for her, my responses, verbal and non-verbal, must have reassured her. My questions came only when she seemed at a loss as to what to say next and I sat in a position where she could see my face easily if she wanted to, but was not confronted by me every time she looked up. Her tension eased considerably as the session went on.

The Client's Story

Lisa began by telling me that she was a teacher, working with five- and six-year-olds. Although she was happy in the classroom and loved the children, she felt desperately ill at ease with the rest of the staff and in social situations generally. I asked her if she could describe this feeling in more detail and she said that she was 'very very shy', 'aware of myself all the time', depressed, lonely, 'what's the point of it all?' She was clearly ashamed at being near to tears but relieved when I handed her some tissues and said that we all needed to cry when things got too much and she need not mind expressing her unhappiness here.

She then described severe panic attacks which occurred particularly during staff meetings at the school. She would find herself becoming tense, breathless, sweating, unable to look at anyone and had the sensation of being outside herself, looking down at what was going on. (I had encountered reports of such depersonalisation experiences associated with panic attacks before, but it was obviously important to listen for other signs that she might be suffering from something even more serious than anxiety.) She never spoke at these staff meetings and if she thought she might be asked to comment on a child, she wanted to run away but was immobilised. She had had a year's break from her training and left after her first year as a qualified teacher because of these experiences, and had returned to the profession some two years previously.

I commented that this sounded very courageous after all she had been through and she said, rather tentatively, that she thought she was probably a good teacher. She liked most of her colleagues, although she was not really close to any of them, and the head teacher in particular she admired for her confidence. Lisa was again thinking of giving up but was reluctant to change to something new and could not face explaining her reasons for leaving. She felt she would be letting down one very needy child in particular, with whom she had established an especially warm relationship. It would also mean running away yet again.

I asked Lisa about the rest of her life. She had a bed-sitting-room in a house with other women, mostly students, all younger than herself. She hardly knew the others, except for one, Carol, who was her closest friend. She had a few other friends and was quite close to one of her three sisters who lived nearby. She went out with them occasionally but mostly stayed at home in the evenings, preparing her lessons for the next day or reading. She was happiest just sitting talking with Carol. There she felt at ease and confident in herself. I asked her what this feeling was like in contrast to the more stressful situations? She was relaxed and open, loved to talk and hear about Carol's day and be able to laugh for a change!

I noticed that Lisa had so far made little mention of her family and I asked her about them. Apart from the sister living in London, the rest lived in Scotland – her father, two elder sisters and a brother. Her mother had died when she was 12 years old. Lisa looked away at this point, flushed and fell silent. I asked her gently whether she remembered that time. She said no, she felt that she had lost her some years before that when her mother started to drink very heavily. (As this was agreed to be simply an initial meeting, I did not explore this obviously threatening area further.) Her father had been more responsible for the children's upbringing, she thought. He was 'careful' for them, made sure that they were warm and fed, but had strict rules and was 'remote'. As a child she had been seen as 'the nervous one' and treated as the baby, although she was 18 months older than the sister in London. She never had many friends but tended to rely on one special relationship at school. She had left Scotland at the age of 19 to train as a teacher.

Were there any other aspects of her life she thought important? 'Yes – men!' We both laughed at the sudden exasperated explosion. But this too was obviously an area of unhappiness for her and I asked her seriously what her experience was. Relationships with three men had followed a very similar pattern. Each time she had dropped everything for the man concerned, devoted herself to him to the extent that she began to resent being 'a doormat' and ended the relationship when she felt that she might be rejected. It seemed that she predicted disaster each time and each time her predictions were validated (a clear example of hostility). She had not realised until I asked that the ending of these relationships coincided with an increase in her anxiety attacks and breaks in her career. The last man she had shared a flat with up until she left him two months previously.

The Initial Contract

Lisa glanced at the clock and blushed again when we had been talking for about 40 minutes. I said that we still had at least ten minutes left and asked her what she hoped for from counselling. She knew what she wanted: to be happier, not so aware, to cope with things better, be a better teacher, form a special relationship but 'sort myself out first'. What she did not know was how to set about it all. I asked her why the personal construct approach appealed to her and she said that she liked the emphasis on the person's own views and the idea that it was possible to change if 'you saw things in a way which wasn't helping you'. She had felt relieved to talk to me and wanted to embark on a series of counselling sessions.

Her friend had shown her a self-characterisation and a rated grid she had completed (see Chapter 4) and Lisa expressed an interest in both. I agreed that they could be very helpful in pin-pointing issues more clearly. I suggested that we meet for four further sessions to begin with, as this would give us time to explore how she saw herself and her world through these and other procedures and reach some understanding of what change might involve for her. I then gave her the instructions for writing a self-characterisation (see Chapter 4, p. 57) and she said that she would post it to me before the first of these sessions.

As we walked down the stairs I told her how much I enjoyed working with young children and looked forward to hearing more about her approach to a whole class, as I, on the whole, saw them one at a time with their mothers. It seemed important to end with reference to what seemed to be one of the few areas in which she felt some satisfaction with herself.

THE COUNSELLOR'S FIRST IMPRESSIONS

As always, I had left time after the session to reflect on our meeting. I held the image of her as she sat, tense and nervous at first, gradually sitting back more easily in her chair as she found that I listened and accepted what she had to say without judgement of any kind. I had a strong sense that she felt very threatened by her own openness to me, but was touched by the aggression which led her to tell so much. Here was someone, I felt, who really wanted to work on her difficulties, despite fears of her own inadequacy. What might this work involve? I made some notes on a number of factors which should be borne in mind as likely to contribute to a transitive diagnosis (see Chapter 3, p. 35).

The need to access pre-verbal construing
It seems that Lisa is stuck in a pattern of relationships (with men and women) where she becomes intensely dependent on a 'best friend' or lover. But her hostility is such that she has to *make* the relationship fail. It is likely that such a pattern remains at a pre-verbal level of construing and we will need at some point to explore her early experiences of her parents and siblings to find out why she cannot be the sort of person who succeeds in relationships. However, I predict, from the way she spoke and blushed as she referred to them, that this will be too threatening immediately and indeed might well not be attempted in these exploratory sessions. The feelings of anger and deprivation which seem to be masked by doubts about herself in later relationships might be overwhelming at this point. Only by bringing such experience to a higher level of awareness, however, can she have the freedom to disperse her dependencies more widely and elaborate her core roles.

Her experience of anxiety at staff meetings is undoubtedly linked to her hostility in ensuring the breakdown of her relationships, and it will be essential to explore their meaning more fully. What is it that makes these everyday events so hard for her to construe? What are the links between these experiences and experiences of the past which render her so helpless in the face of them? I can only, at this stage, construe something of the intensity of her panic.

Areas of potential movement and signs of aggression
Positive prognostic indicators are signs of potential movement and some evidence of her dealing with problems aggressively. Although Lisa has always been considered the baby of the family she nevertheless left home and came to London to train as a teacher. Although she has twice given up her career she has had the courage to try again. Her view of herself as a teacher is a positive one in relation to the children despite her lack of role in relation to the other members of staff. And coming for counselling, instead of giving herself up as a bad job, suggests a real determination to 'sort herself out'. Making her aware of the resources she undoubtedly possesses will be a major thrust of the reconstruing process to develop some core roles.

Areas of constraint
At the moment, Lisa does not seem to construe herself as an adult person in her own right. She 'functions' well as a teacher in one context, but hopelessly in others. As both lover and friend she relates in a child-like way. From her references to others, it seems she probably has some quite constellatory views on how she *should* be in all three areas of her life and finds herself lacking. Living as she does in one room in a house with much younger people gives her evidence that she has achieved nothing since her student days. Her sparse social life and limited interests must add to her sense of inadequacy and constriction.

The types of construction used in different areas
When Lisa spoke of her work with the children she showed a rich discrimination in her perceptions of them. When she spoke of the teachers, however, her construing became tighter and more restricted: they were, naturally, *confident*, *bright* and *able to relate well to one another*. Social situations for her, especially in a large group, are seen almost entirely in terms of the anxiety and threat they hold for her. Reference to her family focused mainly on the dependency issues involved. Comments on herself placed her firmly on the non-preferred poles of her constructs, with only a few exceptions. We shall probably need to loosen her construing in these areas. But I shall have to subsume her construing better to discover the means for doing this.

With these impressions in mind, I now needed to make a more systematic exploration of the major themes governing her view of life and the processes involved in her construing of events during the four sessions we had agreed upon. Only then would it be possible to tighten up on the formulation of the first transitive diagnosis.

EXPLORING LISA'S WORLD

The Self-characterisation

I received the following character sketch from Lisa before we met again.

Lisa is 28 and works as a teacher. She is not very tall, a little plump in the wrong places and not very attractive. She is sensitive and gets upset very easily by what people say. She does not like criticism and becomes very defensive when faced with such situations. She doesn't like to make people feel embarrassed or unhappy. Upsetting people makes her feel insecure.

She makes lots of resolutions about how she is going to be and act towards people, but never keeps to them. She tells people too much about herself and then regrets it. She finds it hard to tell people what she wants and ends up doing things she doesn't want. She spends a lot of time apologising and making excuses for herself, especially with those she doesn't really know.

She doesn't like to show people the bad side of her personality and tries to hide this from friends, but at times the selfishness shows when she is not fully aware of it.

She is very self-oriented, but not because she thinks she is anything important, more she feels people are judging her all the time. She blushes very easily – in groups with peers at work where she can panic and with people she doesn't know, also with men more than women. She likes to work hard to please her colleagues and peers. She enjoys her work most of the time but is sometimes aware that her common sense and perception are not very great.

She can be happy and fun to be with, with close friends. She finds alcohol makes her more relaxed and outgoing towards people she doesn't know.

She is kind and helpful to her friends and is always pleased when they show their appreciation or value her opinion. She also likes to do things for fun and is happy when they need her. She sometimes feels good about herself but these times are rare and depend on so many other things in her life at the time. At times she enjoys being on her own but only in familiar surroundings. She doesn't like change. This is when she faces up and sees her inadequacies very clearly.

Analysis of Lisa's self-characterisation   This sketch both confirmed some of my first impressions and added to my understanding of how she saw herself. It also raised a number of questions I needed to keep in mind.

As we have said (Chapter 4), Kelly suggests we start our analysis of a self-characterisation by looking at the opening and closing sentences. Here Lisa begins with comments on her age, occupation and looks – she is 'not very attractive'. She ends with her fear of change and sense of her inadequacy. All in all, therefore, inside and out, she does not think much of herself.

A number of important themes emerge. She has a feeling of being judged. She wishes to please others and fears upsetting them. This only validates her construing of herself as an inadequate person. She makes resolutions but is unable to follow them through. (Would this apply to her involvement in counselling?) She tells people too much about herself, although wanting to hide the 'bad' side of her personality (perhaps she was regretting having told me so much). Although able to say something favourable about being fun to be with and occasionally feeling good about herself, this is overshadowed by the inadequacies which dominate the account. It is interesting that she makes so little of the distressing attacks at staff meetings. Perhaps she simply construes them at the moment as symbolising her general feeling of helplessness and cannot elaborate further?

Lisa does not place herself in a particular context or role and mentions others in terms of 'friends' or 'peers' rather than as specific people. This seems to underline the feeling of isolation and the constriction I had sensed from her account of her life. There is no mention of her family or her past or of the later relationships she spoke of at the first meeting. Either her focus is very much in the present or, as seemed likely when she spoke of it, the past is too threatening to consider at this stage. Her current view of her world is reduced to her own shortcomings and the assumed responses of others towards her.

When Lisa arrived for the first of our four exploratory sessions she immediately asked whether her 'writing' had arrived and whether what she had written was what I wanted. I thanked her for giving me plenty of time to go through it and said that I'd found it very helpful. We went through the self-characterisation together and agreed on the main issues presented in it. When I asked her whether she had regretted having told so much last time she said 'no', she had felt safe afterwards and reaffirmed the relief she expressed at the time. She herself had realised that she had not mentioned her family and wondered whether she 'ought' to have done. As predicted, she spoke with some fear of having to talk about her parents. I assured her that nothing would be forced on her and she explained that she had warm memories of her mother from very early times – it was as if she had blotted out the period of years before her death when she was not herself and she clearly did not wish at this stage to stir up memories of what must have been distressing for her. In fact subsequent events showed that she was not ready to address her feelings about her mother for quite a long time.

A Rated Grid

I now wanted to explore the processes involved in Lisa's construing in a more structured way, so I proposed that we begin to look at how she saw people in general, as well as herself, along the lines of Kelly's introduction of grid procedure to his client quoted in Chapter 4 (p. 68). Lisa was enthusiastic about it because of the grid her friend had shown her and towards the end of that first session we began eliciting constructs, largely through the triadic method described earlier. The second and third sessions were mainly devoted to further eliciting and laddering of constructs, with Lisa elaborating her views of friends, family and her relationships with the men in her life as she went along.

She chose as elements (see Chapter 4) her three sisters (Alice, Kate and Margaret), her brother (John), her father, the headmistress of her current school (Angela), four female friends (Carol, Toni, Jane and Chris) and her ex-boyfriend (Ray). In order to ensure a range of people, I asked her to include someone she felt sorry for (Paul) and someone whom she felt uneasy with (Beryl). When I suggested also someone she admired she said that Angela was the person she admired most. Someone whom she felt knew what he wanted was Jack. In addition, as it seemed important to clarify the ways in which she wanted to change, she agreed to include 'Me as I am Now' and 'Me as I'd Like to Be'. She did not at first include her mother but agreed to do so on my suggestion, saying that it seemed wrong to pretend she hadn't existed.

The constructs were partly elicited by the triadic method described earlier (p. 63), some of which were then laddered. One or two were taken from her self-characterisation and, not surprisingly, some of them emerged from both contexts. Lisa had little difficulty in rating the constructs on a seven-point scale, although she had some hesitation in committing more negative ratings to paper. She did not like 'judging' people, any more than she liked to be judged herself, as she had written.

By the fourth session I had analysed the grid using Higginbottom and Bannister's GAB programme referred to briefly in Chapter 4 (p. 73). We saw there how both constructs and elements are grouped together according to their correlations with one another.

Figure 6.1 shows the main closely related group of elements or people in Lisa's grid. She was surprised to find 'Jane' emerging as the leading element, as she was not the friend Lisa felt she knew best. I asked her whether perhaps Jane represented most strongly the qualities which this group had in common and this made sense to her. It can be seen that a number of her friends, two of her sisters and the headmistress, 'Angela', are highly related to 'Me as I'd Like to Be'. (The figures show the correlations between these elements and 'Jane'.) 'Me Now' is seen as significantly different from them all. A considerable distance such as here between 'Me Now' and 'Me as I'd Like to Be' has been found to occur in the grids of people who are depressed. The sense of isolation which was conveyed both as she told her story and in her self-characterisation is highlighted in this aspect of her

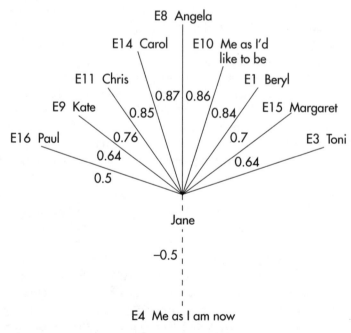

FIGURE 6.1 *Main cluster of elements in Lisa's grid*

grid. And Lisa's construing of many other people so positively looked as if it played its part in keeping herself down.

Figure 6.2 shows the main group of constructs in Lisa's grid. The leading one, *no staying power* as opposed to *follows things through*, is the construct which has the greatest number of other constructs highly correlated with it, positively or negatively. In psychological terms Lisa is saying that people who have no staying power (that is, Lisa herself) are also *self-oriented, shy, inadequate, apologetic, feel vulnerable to judgement*, are *not caring*, are *unsure/holding back*, *show their feelings too much* and *don't come over as interesting*.

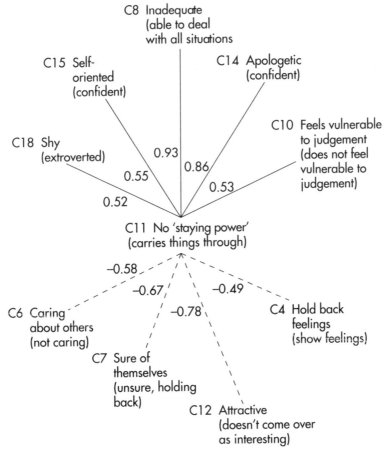

FIGURE 6.2 *Main cluster of constructs in Lisa's grid*

These were the main aspects of the grid discussed with Lisa during our fourth session. She found that there were 'no surprises', but felt clearer about where she was and what she needed to work on. In her terms, this amounted to her 'terrible self-image' and the need to make more of her life. She very much wanted to carry on with the counselling and, while I could not specify 'how long it would take' I suggested that we work together on a weekly basis until the end of her summer term (that is, for twelve sessions) and then review the situation. Lisa was happy with that suggestion.

Transitive Diagnosis

I now felt in a better position to tighten up my construing of Lisa's view of herself and her situation by formulating a transitive diagnosis. This would serve as a basis for our initial work. I again found it helpful to clarify my thoughts in writing my notes:

> Lisa has become trapped by developing ways of construing herself which set her apart and make her different from others. In a sense, this system is constellatory in nature: 'I am Lisa, therefore I can only be . . .'. Her attempts to form intense relationships may be seen as hostile. They have to fail because she would not be able to cope with the resulting threat and guilt of their succeeding.

In this regard her problem was much like Trixibell's (see Chapter 2). But they differ in a number of major respects. Trixibell's problem was essentially at a pre-verbal level centring on dependency and manifesting itself in disturbed relationships and psychosomatic symptoms. Lisa's can be viewed more usefully as a failure to develop a bi-polar construing of 'self'. She has only elaborated herself at one pole of her construing system and has therefore denied herself room to manoeuvre.

> Her panic at staff meetings can be seen as an awareness that she has all the skills needed to play a full part, but that very awareness brings her face to face with 'nothingness' – she has no way of construing herself as the sort of person who can cope as the others do.
>   The way forward therefore is three-fold. (1) To change the nature of her construing of self from constellatory to propositional (from her current rigid, unchanging view of herself to one which would allow her more scope and potential). (2) To work at some of the inconsistencies

within her construing system which help maintain the status quo and contribute to the panic attacks. (Both 1 and 2 involve encouraging loosening.) (3) At the same time to help her elaborate her alternative self and, thereby, core roles. As this is done, her panic attacks should decrease.

An essential ingredient in all this clearly needed to be a reduction in the hostility with which Lisa had maintained her position so far. The suggestions for this process put forward in Chapter 5 (p. 104) relate closely to the above aims. With a loosening of her self-construing, the clarification of inconsistencies and the elaboration of an alternative self, the 'feelings of chaos' which are at their most acute during panic attacks should give way to a greater sense of control and leave her open to 'opportunities for aggressive explorations'.

STAGE ONE OF THE COUNSELLING PROCESS

Clarification of Lisa's Construing

Before embarking on a plan of action involving other people, there were some aspects of Lisa's construing which needed further clarification as they were clearly contributing to the position in which she found herself. There seemed to be one or two possible confusions or contradictions which might usefully be unravelled, a process which, in itself, should provide the means for gentle initial loosening.

First we looked at her construct of *closed* versus *outgoing, open* more carefully, as she seemed to have recurrent problems with it. Using the ABC model (see p. 65) a dilemma was clearly revealed:

Peggy: Which would you prefer to be, closed or outgoing and open?
Lisa: Outgoing and open really.
Peggy: Why do you choose that side? What are the advantages?
Lisa: Well, then people accept you. Or they're more likely to.
Peggy: So what are the disadvantages of being closed?
Lisa: If you're closed people don't take time to get to know you – so – so they can't accept you, can they?
Peggy: Can you think of any possible *dis*advantages to being outgoing and open, though?
Lisa: [*after a long pause*] People can know you then and judge you.

Peggy: Are there any advantages to being closed?

Lisa: If you're closed people can't judge you as much – they can't see what you're like.

This may be summarised as follows:

A	*closed*	*outgoing, open*
B	(disadvantage)	(advantage)
	people don't take time to get to know you	people accept you
C	(advantage)	(disadvantage)
	people can't judge you so much	people know you and judge you

According to Lisa's theory, therefore, if you are open you are judged, if you are closed people ignore you. Although she chose *outgoing, open* initially, being 'known' could cause unbearable anxiety.

Pre-verbal Aspects of Anxiety

I asked her whether she could relate this to her attacks of panic at staff meetings. She could not immediately make a connection and I encouraged her to try to recall what seemed to her to be their origin. She thought back to her own junior school days some years before her mother's death. She had painful memories of the mockery of one particular teacher, who seemed continually to 'judge' her for her timidity and tearfulness. She remembered being made to stand on her chair, frozen with fear and humiliation. She had felt unable to talk to her mother about it, her father was too remote, her siblings reaffirmed that she was a baby.

It seemed important to give Lisa space to reflect on all this and we sat in silence for a while. I felt that her experience now at her present school was the helplessness of that frightened child. She was threatened by 'the imminent comprehensive change' in her sense of herself when being called upon to be a competent adult. She was also overwhelmed by the anxiety of not being able to make sense of what was happening to her. If she were 'known' as she felt she was at these moments it would be as someone foolish, showing herself in her ignorance to be uncaring about the children and in short a thoroughly 'bad' person, not fit to be a teacher. After a pause I put this to her as a possible interpretation and she said that it 'felt right'. As she knew herself to be well thought of by her colleagues, there was some hostility in this fear, but at this stage Lisa really did consciously believe herself to be inadequate in almost every respect. Only being *sensitive* as opposed to *not thinking about the effect she had on others* seemed to save her.

As this construct also seemed something of a trap we explored that too. Looking at the first paragraph of her self-characterisation it seemed clear that *sensitive* held two different meanings: there was the awareness of others' feelings and the wish not to hurt them and there was her own tendency to be easily upset. The first she valued in herself, the second she found of no use at all. So it seemed important to separate the two constructs. She did this by finding a new opposite to *hypersensitive* which she relabelled for the type of sensitivity related only to herself. There were a number of alternatives she might have chosen. She considered *thick skinned*, which she disliked, or *tough*, which was not much better. I asked her whether it might not have something to do with not being easily hurt. She said that *able to manage hurt* seemed to be something to work on. This was not just an intellectual exercise. Lisa tested it out a little later at school and found that she had some resources such as humour to help her deal better with possible hurt.

The Counsellor's Role So Far

Although we have spoken of 'partnership' in a joint venture as essential to a personal construct approach to counselling, it will be clear that the relationship itself changes and grows along with other change and growth. And it is an important part of our work to reflect on our own role as the series proceeds. At this stage, Lisa was much more dependent than she was later to become on guidance from me. I drew her attention to inconsistencies in her construing, selected areas which we might work on, being careful to approach those which would be least threatening to her first. And in these early sessions, I suggested possible courses of action in the light of my understanding of her difficulties in relating to people and of the resources she had shown herself to possess. She needed time and encouragement to develop and trust her own inventiveness. This, after all, is a 'good' quality and therefore not 'her'.

Preparation for sessions with her entailed, above all, my trying to predict from what she had said, written and shown in her non-verbal behaviour, what she might make of any experiments that suggested themselves as potentially useful. It was important, for example, for me to begin by placing the emphasis on more discriminating observation of events and people, rather than plunge her into active changes in her own behaviour. Any attempts to elaborate new roles in life would need to be made from a basis of a more positive valuation of those she already had. For the time being, I simply had to accept as true for her her construing of herself as vulnerable and dependent throughout her life.

STAGE TWO: THE PLAN OF ACTION

Apart from the issues clarified above, Lisa felt that the self-characterisation and the grid together gave a clear impression of how she felt about her situation and we made our first plans for experimentation. There seemed to be three main areas for work at this stage:

1 Making the constellatory nature of her negative construing of self in comparison with others more propositional (i.e. encouraging more varied predictions of her own and others' dealings with life.)
2 Exploring some of the non-verbalised areas of her construing of her 'self' in order to find an alternative to panic.
3 Elaborating alternative aspects of the self.

Construing Others

For the first area, I needed to help Lisa set about construing others more fully rather than attempting to boost her own image. This was not to force her to pull down all these admirable people from their pedestals but to enquire whether they too might not be human. This entailed not only considering just how confident, coping and outgoing they all were but applying a wider range of constructs to them. She needed to develop greater sociality (to 'construe the construction processes' of others), put herself in others' shoes, before she could play a more effective social role with respect to them. I asked her to write sketches of a number of people, imagining them in different situations and, when she thought about it, she was able to say that they too might sometimes feel ill at ease and even occasionally be selfish in some ways. In terms of vulnerability in particular she came to realise that the headmistress, Angela, whom she admired for her confidence and ability to carry things through, probably could be hurt. I had asked her to write the following sketch of her as if she were Angela writing her own self-characterisation.

Most people see Angela as a competent, confident and cheerful person who does her demanding job well and is able to run a home at the same time. She *is* competent, but not as unshakeable in her confidence as she appears. Although she is open to question she can be hurt by unfair criticism from parents, for example, or when one of the staff seems to want to block some plan she has for improvement.

She is on the whole happily married to Stephen but she sometimes wishes that he realised that she too needs support and comfort occasionally. She does spend a lot of her time listening to his worries about work. Although he is proud of her success in her career, he doesn't really want to know about the day to day events in school. They probably bore him. But he is mostly loving and she knows that she is lucky to have him.

She would like to have children of her own but is afraid that it may be too late.

This sketch suggested that Lisa had observed Angela with some care and had perceived some possible areas of difficulty for her and aspects of her relationship with her husband which were less than perfect. I wondered, though, whether her statement that Angela would feel herself 'lucky to have him' might not be an interpretation through her own construing system and, when challenged, she agreed. She added that she had no idea whether Angela wanted children of her own and was sure that she was talking about herself at this point. This realisation seemed to be an important step towards greater sociality, which would help her to see people more clearly as they might be. She did, indeed, become a perceptive observer of colleagues and friends and less and less inclined to measure herself against them. As time went on, this had the effect of making her construe herself as well as others in a more open and variable way.

Experiencing Anxiety

Perhaps Lisa's most difficult task was to change the way she experienced anxiety at school meetings. Being able to remember something of her experience all those years ago gave some meaning to the events – the helplessness of the frightened child, the fear of being known for what she felt she still was in these situations. Somewhere, however, there was an alternative self – a child who refused to stand on her chair and weep, an adult who stood up for herself, rather than running away from a relationship as an alternative to being a doormat. What was so threatening about that other possible self? I suspected that it had something to do with the anger she felt towards her parents, her siblings, that tormenting teacher, her lovers, which at the time she had found too frightening to express, choosing, rather, to be helpless. With so much still unexplored with regard to those earlier experiences, it was important to limit the implications of any change in the school situation to that context alone.

We therefore focused the discussion on her humiliation as a child at school as a crucial reason for her fear of 'teachers'. She was able to acknowledge something of her 'hatred' of the woman concerned as we spoke of her again. Her work on construing her colleagues more fully should make it more possible to relate to them as the real and varied people that they were at such times. She already had a notion of herself as 'a good teacher' when she was in the classroom. Could she be that aspect of herself in the context of the staff room, where she was, after all, equally concerned with the welfare of the children? When we discussed this, Lisa said that she never thought of the children at all at these times. It was as if she 'went back years'. She would try to 'stay in her teacher role'.

I asked her, first, to focus her attention on listening to what others were saying, without attempting to take part. This was hard but the effort of switching the focus of her awareness outside herself began to bear fruit. From listening she moved to trying to gauge what they were feeling about the issues they discussed and how they saw things. This took her even further from the preoccupation with herself and she gradually began spontaneously to join in. One morning she knew that the little girl she had befriended was to be discussed and, although afraid, she was so concerned to put her case she 'forgot herself' when it came to it and spoke out at some length.

The change occurring here in Lisa's experience is essentially one from extreme constriction (or narrowing of focus), where all she can construe is her physical sensation of fear, to a gradual dilation (or widening of view). She is able not only to expand her perception of herself but to bring other people within the range of her attention. In a state of constriction, all she can predict is imminent 'falling to pieces'. Later, becoming more aware of the situation as a whole, she is able to make predictions and respond on the basis of an understanding of what is going on.

Relating to Others: the Use of Enactment

Alongside such experiments we were looking at alternative ways of relating to those on whom she was more dependent, such as her close male and female friends. It seemed to me that we could not get too far with this without going into her relationship with her parents and she did begin to speak more of her father. She obviously regretted the distance between himself and all his children and wondered how she could get closer to him. At first she felt she had no idea how to talk to him, so we experimented with different ways of approaching him through enactment. By reversing roles, each of us portraying both herself and her father in the same 'scenes', she could explore the nature of the threat to herself in embarking on such conversations and gain some understanding of how he might feel as she put herself in his shoes. In our first attempts, she pleaded with him for reassurance, begged him to talk to her. As Lisa, I expressed something of the anger as well as the hurt she must have felt and she was gradually able to do the same.

She went home as often as she could and tried to talk to him more about the past as well as what was happening at present. He too apparently was unwilling to speak much of her mother but he did tell her something of how it was for him after she died. Although she felt she understood how difficult it must have been for him, at the same time, the feelings of anger both at being treated as the baby by her sisters and 'neglected' by her father were even stronger than during our enactments. She found this painful at first as it seemed to imply judgement of him. But when she was able to accept as real both her early feelings towards him and her current understanding of him she found it liberating rather than threatening.

Tightening the Construing of What was Taking Place

This work took place over a period of about three months. At this stage, with so much going on, I felt that it was important to tighten her construing by reviewing where she was. Apart from the developments described, I pin-pointed with Lisa signs of general dilation and aggression (a widening of her view of possibilities and active steps to enhance her experience). She was planning to move out of her bed-sitter and share a flat with her sister. She got on reasonably well with her but there was certainly some anticipation of difficulties between them. She also decided to apply for a post at a new school which carried more responsibility with it as the children who went there often came from disturbed backgrounds. She wanted the job very much but knew she would be risking 'judgement' and might have to deal with rejection. She had begun to initiate social contacts more instead of waiting to be asked out and had gone out alone more than once. We had spent some time in considering how she might enhance her life more generally, as a result of which she had signed on for a language course in the summer and hoped to join a badminton club in the autumn.

One real threat in all this stood out for her which related to her unresolved dependency problems. If she left the house and shared with her sister, would she lose the closeness to her friend Carol? She was already feeling jealous of Carol's relationship with another girl and felt that she might be ousted from her affections if she moved on. Lisa spoke of this jealousy and possessiveness with some shame and of her earlier jealousy in relation to boyfriends. At school she had apparently always had one special close friend and always 'lost' her at some stage, which caused her great pain and depression even at the age of seven. At this stage the threat was simply acknowledged but again it seemed clear that there was unfinished business.

After a short break for her summer holidays we met at three-weekly intervals during the autumn term to consolidate the changes she had made. By this time the anxiety attacks had become a thing of the past, she had moved into the flat with her sister and had dealt well with disappointment. She had not been offered the post at the new school. She was surprised herself at how well she took this. But although clearly sorry, she did not seem to feel rejected and did not become depressed. As it turned out she was offered promotion at her own school which made her feel that at last she was 'following things through'.

At this stage we both felt that a break would be beneficial. It was clear that there was more work to do in the area of dependency but it seemed appropriate for her to develop what she had done so far on her own for a while. She was to contact me when she needed to or felt ready to look at other issues.

STAGE THREE

Lisa contacted me six months later. She was planning to buy a flat of her own. Could she cope alone? She had applied for a place on a course for working with disturbed children. Would she follow it through? She had developed one or two friendships with men but felt afraid to commit herself to another close relationship. At the same time the wish to be married and have children was very strong. There were problems with her father, who had become quite ill and she was at a loss as to what to do. There was clearly much threat as newly formed constructs about herself were being put to the test.

Evaluating Change and Possibilities for Further Movement

We agreed it would be useful at this point to do another grid to see where Lisa was now and what further changes might be projected. It was debatable whether she should rerate the old constructs to give a more direct comparison or elicit some more constructs to show a different kind of change. She chose the former, but substituted one or two of the elements for people whom she had come to know since last year.

Comparing her ratings of the 'Self Now' we found a considerable difference between the two grids. In the second grid she rated herself more favourably on quite a few of the constructs, although giving herself the central position on a number of them showed her to be very much in transition. She saw herself as less *sensitive* largely due to the work she had done earlier on her hypersensitivity about herself. Additionally, though, she had come to question whether being so concerned with not upsetting others was such a good thing. They too had humour and could cope. She was less vulnerable, more sure of herself and not so shy. Instead of 'Me Now' being negatively correlated with 'Me as I'd Like to Be', the correlation was positive, although quite low at 0.39. She still had a way to go in her own eyes. 'Me as I'd Like to Be', she felt, was 'more realistic' the second time round.

Another self-characterisation written at this time underlines all this. Whereas the first sketch ends with her fears about change, the main theme of the second is the elaboration of how much she feels she has changed. She is much less easily upset, relating more easily to colleagues and a wider circle of friends. She is more confident in her role as a teacher. She expresses her concern about her father but refers to plans for herself and her own need to move on.

The Changing Role of the Counsellor

Lisa undoubtedly brought greater resources to this second phase of our work and my role in it consequently changed. I was still, of course, in a better position than she to notice inconsistencies in her construing. There were to be times when, by resisting the temptation to 'mother' her in her distress, I was able to validate her growing sense of herself as an adult. But she was now able to make links between her current reactions to events and past experience. She could anticipate possible difficulties and make more effective choices as to how to meet them. She took a more active part in drawing up a new plan of action.

The New Plan of Action

The aims were:

1   to reduce the anxiety about living alone by elaborating Lisa's expectations and plans, thus making the event more predictable;
2   to reduce the anxiety and threat around the new course by elaboration of expectations and study planning;
3   to explore further unverbalised aspects of the 'self' and address her basic dependency problems more fully.

These aims were not worked through in order, but gradually and concurrently as they came to the forefront in the ensuing two months.

The least difficult to tackle was her fear of living alone. Sharing with her sister, who lived a very different life and had largely different friends had proved to her that she could plan things by herself and with her own friends. I asked her not only to anticipate the kinds of things she would do, but also how she wanted the new flat to be in some detail. I suggested that she use drawing as well as verbal description here, which Lisa much enjoyed. All this had the effect of grounding her in the reality of some of the implications of the move and took away a good deal of the threat of being alone. She decided that she was, in fact, going to be 'selfish' in contrast to the time when she shared with her last boyfriend and had no say in matters at all. She turned out to have very imaginative as well as practical ideas and she clearly took great pleasure in setting up her new home. There were no problems of loneliness. She had come to enjoy entertaining and also enjoyed being on her own there.

Her fears about following through the course seemed mainly to do with doubts about her ability to study and we approached this by setting up a course of reading around subjects well before the course started. She also attended some lectures at the local Evening Institute. When she did begin the course the following autumn she adjusted very well and followed through to her new qualification.

The issues around her father's growing dependency were much harder for her to deal with. Although she had reached a far greater understanding of her early experience of him, a change in him brought out some new aspects of their relationship. After a severe illness she felt that he had become almost child-like and very demanding in expecting his daughters, especially herself, to come to spend much more time at home and organise everything for him. Lisa was willing to do her share but resented her younger sister's apparent lack of interest and her eldest sister's 'excuse' (being newly married) for not doing very much for him. In fact she was very distressed by the amount of thoroughly negative emotions aroused in her and wondered whether she had become a much more wicked person or had been hiding such feelings from herself all these years. She was envious of her married sister, deeply angry with her father and beginning to question the source of her mother's unhappiness and deterioration. It was a great deal to bear.

The Threat of Loosening

Lisa had clearly tightened in the face of all this. It seemed timely to attempt some gentle loosening. Relaxation was established at the beginnings of sessions and she put it into practice in the evenings when she got home. This enabled her to be more open to early feelings about her parents and she began to remember her dreams for the first time. In some of them her mother featured as a victim of some unkindness from her father, in some of them she herself was ill treated by him and in the worst both her parents were cold and dismissive towards her. Only in one did she feel that she stood up for herself and showed her anger towards them. From all the others she woke up weeping. Lisa was very upset by these dreams and went through a phase of believing that they were the 'real truth'. She became angry with me and for a short time seemed to see me also as some kind of cold parental figure. During one session she declared herself at the end of her tether and thought she ought to grit her teeth, go back to Scotland and look after her father for the rest of his life. It was all she deserved. Understandably, Lisa had retreated to a position of hostility. She had ample proof that she was 'no good' after all.

Although this was a difficult time for Lisa, the change in her was not as worrying as it might appear. I resisted the temptation to protect her from threat by diverting to a 'safer' area as I felt that she had now elaborated herself positively enough to deal with it. It seemed that instead of her old depression and immobilisation she was now fully experiencing a lot of feelings she had not been in touch with before and being aggressive in taking the risk of expressing them. But she needed to tighten again to some extent in order to move forward. She was at a time of very important choices.

> *Peggy*: This is perhaps one of the most difficult moments of choice you've ever reached. Shall we look at just what your options seem to be?
>
> *Lisa*: That might help.
>
> *Peggy*: You could go back to Scotland, live with your father and look after him. What would that mean for you?
>
> *Lisa*: Back to square one, I suppose. The unselfish one – the doormat.
>
> *Peggy*: And that won't do?
>
> *Lisa*: No – it won't do. I *can't* go backwards.
>
> *Peggy*: Right. Then you could wash your hands of it all and get on with your own life.
>
> *Lisa*: I'd feel too guilty. He *is* my father and he did his best for us when mother couldn't cope.
>
> *Peggy*: What other alternatives are there?
>
> *Lisa*: God knows.
>
> *Peggy*: I'm wondering why it's all down to you. Why you feel that you have to take all the responsibility here.
>
> *Lisa*: I suppose because I've always been the one who couldn't take responsibility and it's about time I did. I can't stay a child all my life. I've got to grow up sometime.
>
> *Peggy*: Aren't there other grown-ups involved? Your sisters, your brother, your father himself? Does anyone really know what he wants? Does he know, do you think?
>
> *Lisa*: Probably not.
>
> *Peggy*: Hadn't you better find out? And even if he doesn't know what he wants you might think again about what your share in all this might be.

Lisa decided to invite her father down to London, enlisting her younger sister's help in looking after him. He did not know what he wanted; he only felt that the girls 'owed' him something. And he could not wait to get back home, although he now lived virtually in squalor, with broken-down heating and a leaking roof. Full of frustration and much sadness Lisa got all the family together and with admirable organisation worked out a plan of shared responsibility. Between them they made the house habitable again and they offered their father a kind of rota of attendance and visits. This seemed to appeal to his sense of justice and things settled down reasonably well.

Construing Dependency

This still left the area of dependency around Lisa's mother, which seemed to be implicated in her later relationships. Through the dreams she had had she was rather more in touch with her feelings about her mother. They were clearly ambivalent, swinging from the sense of being deprived of love to a real concern for what her mother might have suffered. Lisa had clung to her memories of early warmth and happiness and now wondered whether these were all fantasy. The only way to alleviate the anxiety which arose through this doubt in her mind seemed to me for her to take the risk of checking it out. She had spoken little of these times with her siblings and I encouraged her to share something of her feelings with them. Her memories were to a large extent confirmed when she spoke at last to the eldest of her sisters. Alice remembered both the better times and the period of change in their mother. To her, the beginning of their mother's drinking was linked with the death of her own mother, with whom she had had a very difficult relationship. The formidable old lady had apparently disapproved of her son-in-law and her daughter had been torn between them for many years. When the grandmother died she seemed to withdraw from her husband and her children and we can only speculate as to the guilt involved there.

All this began to make some sense to Lisa and she could accept the connection I made between her own intense dependency on friends and lovers and the withdrawal of her mother's love. According to her sister, Lisa had turned to her father at this time and he was unable to respond to her needs. The loss of his wife caused him to withdraw too. The question now was whether she had to continue with this pattern, to remain the victim of her biography. She wondered why she of all the children had been the one to experience her parents' withdrawal as personal rejection. It was likely that her role as baby of the family and her elder sisters' attitude, or what she made of these things, contributed a good deal to this difficulty with dependency.

For the next few weeks Lisa was 'quiet in herself' but no longer depressed. She had not a great deal to say during the sessions, which contained long periods of silence that she seemed to need. From time to time she would speak of thinking about her mother in these silences and once she wept and said what a shame it had all been. Although she could not pretend that she now found her father easier to be with, she thought of him too with sadness. She wished she could talk about her mother with him but he turned away when she tried.

Coming to an End

From this time on Lisa came less frequently. Our sessions took the form of 'progress reports', on the course she was involved in, work and social life in general. She did take the risk of a closer relationship with a man and although she felt that the old pattern of preoccupation with him was no longer there, she experienced a good deal of jealousy and suspicion at one stage when they were first considering marriage. She then applied for a job in the Midlands, was accepted and was due to leave London in a few weeks' time. We prepared for our meetings to end, reviewing what had been accomplished and looking forward to her future. She expressed some apprehension but more confidence and seemed to feel that she had achieved more than she had expected when she began. She also believed that there was more change to come.

For our final session I asked her to write down her hopes for the future in the form of a self-characterisation of Lisa in two years' time. She saw herself settled in her new job and enjoying it. She described her family as 'not much changed' but herself as more able to assert herself with her siblings and more tolerant of her ageing father. She hoped that she would be married by then and 'confident enough in herself not to be plagued by jealousy!'. The issue of whether she would have a child by then she left open but when we talked about it she said that she was surprised that it did not seem so vital now as a proof of her worth as a woman.

She herself made comparisons between how she felt now and how she remembered feeling at our first meeting. She recalled her anxiety and the fear of exposing all those inadequacies. She had looked to me as some kind of mother-figure then and recognised how this impression had changed over time as she took more responsibility for what went on. She expressed some sadness at parting but was no longer dependent on seeing me.

For my part, I could quite genuinely say how much I had enjoyed working with her and how much I appreciated the extent to which she had worked for the changes she wanted to make. She knew that she could contact me again if she needed to and said that she would keep me posted as to what happened to her. She kept in regular touch for about a year.

A Christmas card announced that, 'after some ups and downs', she was to be married and her work was going very well.

REFLECTIONS

Lisa undertook 24 sessions of counselling in all over a period of 21 months. She came because of her 'shyness' and the panic attacks experienced at work. It was clear from the beginning that her negative construing of herself was implicated both in failed relationships and the experience of anxiety. The hypothesis that there were also dependency issues involving her view of her parents proved valid as we proceeded. The two self-characterisations and the grids demonstrate the movement she made during the first phase of counselling and in the subsequent period in terms of self-valuation. Her initial experiments for change related to her construing of others more fully and elaborating herself in action as well as thought and feeling. She learned something of sociality and questioned old theories of her own inadequacy.

Only when such groundwork was undertaken did it seem possible for her to address the more basic issues around her dependency on others. By the time she faced her intense feelings about both her parents, she had strengthened her core construing of herself as other than the longing and unsatisfied child. The 'ups and downs' referred to in her last message suggest that forming the relationship she wanted had not been easy. But she seems to have proved herself able to take on the anxiety, threat and guilt inevitably involved in such a process of change.

In our final chapter we shall be looking at aspects of the final stage of the counselling process. We shall consider the implications for ending a series, factors which should be taken into account when bringing it to a close and some ways in which those vital last meetings may be planned. We shall also consider how a period of counselling may feature in the context of the person's life as a whole.

7

ENDING AND EVALUATING THE
PROCESS OF PERSONAL CONSTRUCT
COUNSELLING – AND BEYOND

In Chapter 2 we describe in some detail how the personal construct counsellor prepares for the beginning of a series of meetings. We consider her aims in relation to understanding what the client brings and the client's expectations of the experience. The ending of a period of counselling needs as much, if not more, careful preparation. As at all stages, we need to make predictions about this important part of the process, to ensure that clients are aware of the implications of moving on and able to take into the future the changes in construing which have helped them to overcome current difficulties. Only then may we feel that the aim of this, as of all forms of counselling, has been achieved: to help clients get on the move again and so take full charge of their lives once more.

WHAT ARE THE SIGNS OF SUFFICIENT
PSYCHOLOGICAL MOVEMENT?

So what does the counsellor look for? What are the indications that a client is on the move and ready to live life more effectively? As we have shown, many people who come for help have problems which are more related to the *ways* in which they construe events than the difficulties inherent in those events themselves. As Kelly maintains (1955: 832), 'psychological disorders can be traced to characteristics of a person's construction system' and reconstruction is the most likely means 'for avoiding making the same mistakes in the future'. So it is to these characteristics of the client's construing that we look first for signs that what we set out to do has been accomplished.

Changes in the Nature of the Client's Construing

We have given examples of how extreme tightness or looseness in construing can prevent a person from dealing effectively with others or with life situations. When we can see a client approaching something new with the capacity to loosen their construing to allow for a range of outcomes and then tighten to make some clear predictions as they construe the event, we know that one important aim has been achieved. Mollie, whom we described in Chapter 3 (p. 46) as having trouble with her neighbours, loosened her construing of people generally by making more varying predictions about them initially and only tightened her perception when she got to know them better. Roland's problem was a loosening of his whole system for construing the world that bordered on the type of thought-process disorder found in schizophrenia. He tightened sufficiently to start planning his future and moved towards getting his first ever full-time job.

In Chapter 3 (pp. 48-9) we saw how, in different ways, Mary and Jeremy had difficulty with making decisions. Although this was not all that was wrong in either case, their ability to work through the CPC cycle (circumspection, pre-emption and choice) when faced with something important which had to be decided was one indication that a significant change had taken place. These and many other aspects of a person's construing will have been the main focus of our concern and we look for indications of change in these areas as one criterion for considering termination of counselling.

Coping With Transition

In earlier chapters we have shown how anxiety may be alleviated by helping clients construe events more meaningfully. When they are able to meet new situations in a spirit of enquiry and interest instead of dread and confusion, they too, in this respect at least, are ready to experience things more fully. We looked at aspects of threat and guilt which were invalidating some clients' sense of themselves. When we see that they have become more aware of the implications of change and developed greater resources within themselves, we can have some confidence in their future dealings with life.

We have stressed the importance of helping clients to overcome hostility when threatened with change in some core aspect of their being. We showed how clinging to a personal 'theory' which no longer held good, such as Luke's theory about being a stutterer (Chapter 3, p. 39), immobilised him and, for a time, prevented him reaching his desired goal of fluency. Only when he was able to be more aggressive, to overcome the anxiety of this unfamiliar role of fluent speaker by elaboration of its meaning, could the counsellor (Fay) contemplate ending the series.

OTHER CONSIDERATIONS

Resolving Transference Issues

One very important aspect of the counselling situation which needs to be considered before a series is ended relates to transference, which we discussed in Chapter 5. We suggested there that what Kelly calls 'secondary transference' can be a useful dimension in the process of reconstruction. The client may apply various constructs from figures of the past in his relationship with the counsellor, trying them on for size. The counsellor's validation or invalidation of such constructs may then provide a basis for reorienting the client's constructions of others. The counsellor is incidental to the process.

In 'primary transference', however, the counsellor becomes the central figure in the client's life, a development which Kelly sees as an obstacle to movement. It will be clear that counselling should never end where such a situation remains and the suggestions given for its resolution should be followed well before termination is contemplated.

Changes in Relationship

Even where there are no transference issues to work through, changes in the relationship between client and counsellor may themselves be indicators of the client's readiness to leave. The client becomes less dependent on the counsellor and sets up his own more spontaneous experiments. His world widens and his energies are directed more variously. Such changes are most clearly signalled by changes in the topics discussed. There is a move away from the client's 'problems' and his immediate personal concerns into a more dilated field of interest. Finally he really 'hasn't time' to come any more. Life is too full.

The Client's Life Situation

Although most of the work in a counselling series is to do with change in the client's perception of and approach to events in life, we cannot ignore the fact that many people come to us at a time when their situation is overwhelming by any standards. A person may be experiencing grief and dislodgement through the loss of a child or partner, under serious threat through impending redundancy, suffering the terror and confusion of knowing themselves to be terminally ill. In these circumstances it will be our task to facilitate those reconstructive processes which enable them to approach such events with as much clarity and dignity as possible. The situation itself remains. The timing of the end of counselling may be governed as much by external events as by changes within the person concerned. Continuing support over a long period may be offered.

Even in less extreme instances, it is important to take account of a person's life situation before ending a counselling series. Someone who has had difficulty in relating to others all his life should at least have begun to establish a network of dependencies before he leaves. A woman whose life has been shattered by divorce should have begun to establish new roles for herself. A man who embarks on a totally new pattern of work after being made redundant might do well to share the experiences of transition with the counsellor before going it alone.

Practical Issues

Other factors may, of course, emerge which pre-empt the point at which a period of counselling comes to an end. Practical issues such as time available and proximity to the counsellor may mean that clients have to cut their coat according to their cloth. Counselling can, however, prove useful with only a single or a few sessions available. A set number of sessions may have been agreed upon at the outset and that has to be all, as in some career counselling. Here the choice of what should be worked on and what should be left will be a very sensitive one. But although both client and counsellor may be aware of unsolved problems, there is no reason why the achievement of limited goals should not be valuable.

Phasing Out

Unless there is some such limitation on time, it is unusual for a counselling series to end abruptly after a period of weekly sessions. More often than not a time will come when changes in the client's dealings with life are sufficiently established for fortnightly, then perhaps three-weekly meetings to be appropriate. Finally, as with Lisa in our previous chapter, sessions may occur infrequently and serve as opportunities for reporting on progress. Our account of the final meeting with Lisa shows how such a session may be planned. She was asked to bring a self-characterisation of herself in two years' time to focus on her expectations of the future. There were reflections on the changes that had taken place since counselling began and although she had no qualms about ending the series, it was made clear that she could contact Peggy at any time if she needed to.

The Client's Choice

We have to acknowledge that with personal construct counselling, as with any other, clients may decide not to continue, although the counsellor feels that there is much work to do. The very prospect of change itself may be unconstruable, as with Peter (Chapter 4, p. 58), who saw himself as someone who is 'quite happy just to let events happen and take their own course'. Although none of the client's expectations outlined in Chapter 4 presents insuperable obstacles to counselling, one who is 'looking for support for the problem' may need a good deal of time before such a view can be altered. And the client may not be willing to give that time. One who comes in 'the ultimate state of passivity' *can* be helped but, again, only if she stays long enough for inevitably slow change to take place. Someone wanting an 'instant cure' may try one approach after another and have no more patience with a personal construct counsellor than with any other. In most cases, however, as with Peter, it should be possible to predict from our transitive diagnosis that the person will not follow through.

PLANNING THE END OF COUNSELLING

Whatever the particular circumstances within which client and counsellor begin to look towards the end of a series, it is essential that the counsellor plan both for a review of what has taken place and anticipation of future events in the client's life.

Reviewing the Series

This may be seen as a form of tightening. During an extended period of counselling especially, there will have been a number of review sessions; on completion of some initial meetings to explore the client's problems, for example, or before a break due to holidays. Sometimes, as with Lisa in Chapter 6, a pause seems appropriate to allow the client to develop on her own the changes she has made so far. At all these points, and especially towards the end of a series, a drawing together of the issues worked on and clarification of how things stand are important.

There are a number of ways in which this may be done. Completing the grid used in the early stages of counselling can show changes in the person's perception of themselves and others, together with any loosening or tightening of their construing of people in general. Where the same elements and constructs are used, there is the advantage of a more direct comparison. As we saw, Lisa's self-ratings were a good deal more positive in her second grid and the difference between 'Me Now' and 'Me as I'd Like to Be' much less, showing an increase in her sense of her own worth. If an implications grid has been used initially (see Chapter 4, p. 75), we can look for an increase or decrease in the number of implications for a particular construct. An increase in the number of implications for the client as a fluent speaker and a decrease for the client as a stutterer have been shown to reflect improvement in speech (Fransella, 1972).

Sometimes, however, where the client has clearly dilated her view and is using a wider range of constructs with regard to people or situations, this needs to be highlighted by setting up a new grid, with some of the same elements and constructs perhaps, but with the opportunity to introduce new ones. One young woman, who had come for counselling because of a stammer, chose to leave out 'Me Stammering' and 'Me Fluent' from her second grid a year later, as her speech was no longer of prime importance to her. This, together with a change in a number of other elements, meant a change in the nature of the constructs elicited. They were far less related to issues of being *understood* or whether people were *sensitive* to her problem or not.

Self-characterisations can also be very useful as a method for review. Again, one written at the end of a period of counselling can be compared in detail with one written at the beginning. Jeremy, whose problems with decision-making were referred to in Chapter 3, initially wrote of his frustration at failure in business ventures and in relationships with women. He longed to 'lead a full life', be rich and 'make some kind of impact' at meetings and parties. He had no time for those who 'sat in the corner', risking nothing. Eighteen months later, as he was about to leave counselling, 'success' was still important to him; but he dwelt much more in his writing on the development of closer relationships with friends of both sexes and clearer plans for the career he had at last embarked on. A comparison between the two pieces emphasised the changes he had made in focusing his energies and bringing some kind of order into his formerly chaotic way of life.

There are many ways in which clients may be asked to express their perception of change during a period of counselling. They may simply write down how they see what has occurred and the counsellor may do the same. Similarities and differences between the two accounts may highlight some aspect of the work that they have done together in a way which is useful to both. Ivor, whose firm had sent him to Peggy for a ten-week series of sessions because of 'lack of social and communication skills', gave a typically brisk summary of the factors he had found important in the work we did together:

- Attention to others: eye contact, listening, not interrupting, real interest.
- Conduct of self: relaxation, clear thinking, conservation of mental energy, PHYSICAL WELL-BEING.

The ideas in my version were roughly the same but took up a page and a half. He worked well and, inevitably, learned a good deal about himself and others in the process of becoming a better communicator. I had not realised, though, how seriously he had taken my reference to the need to look after oneself physically when attempting to work more effectively and relate better to others. He saw taking up swimming as a major factor in developing greater awareness of his body, which, in turn, helped him to relax in his relationships with others.

With clients who find drawing a helpful means of expressing themselves, we can sometimes trace the course of change in counselling through pictures made throughout the series. Again, comparing earlier with later ones may convey reconstruction more clearly than words. With the counsellor's sensitivity to non-verbal aspects of a client's behaviour, comparisons between images of them at the first and last meetings form an important part of our perception of change. Veronica, whom we referred to in our section on fixed-role therapy in Chapter 5, not only dressed more attractively as the sessions went on but showed by movement and posture her increased energy and enjoyment of life.

Anticipating the Future

If personal construct counselling aims to get clients on the move again, it is the future we are interested in and what clients may make of their lives. We may, of course, spend much time construing past events, but this is in the interest of what is to come. Before clients leave us it is important, therefore, that those issues reviewed and clarified through the means suggested above are related to events and possibilities in the future. Again, self-characterisations are useful here. A client may be asked to write a sketch of themselves in two, five or ten years time (an example of such is referred to in Chapter 6). From this we can see how far the person is able to look forward in the light of recent experiences. We may if necessary draw their attention to resources in themselves which they are not taking into account.

More specifically, if a future event is known, such as a move to another town or country, a change of job, marriage or the birth of a child or grandchild, we may ask the client to construe its implications. However exciting the prospect may be, there will always be some anxiety and possibly threat in the occurrence which may be reduced by considering alternative outcomes. The greater the change predicted, the more important this process will be.

IS THERE AN ULTIMATE AIM?

Given no specified limit on time and life circumstances which are not in themselves limiting, it may be important to ask ourselves whether there is such a thing as an ultimate goal, an ideal to be striven for. A counsellor working from a personal construct point of view has no prescribed set of interpretations of a person's psychological 'symptoms' and no set formulae for their 'cure'. Equally, there are no beliefs implied in the theory that such or such a way is the best way for a person to conduct themselves and their lives. So what are we aiming for? Until we meet the client and have come to some understanding of what is going wrong, what resources there are for change, we cannot anticipate what might be achieved. Nor can we know how far the clients themselves might be willing to go. We could say that we have fulfilled our joint task when the presenting problem has been resolved. We may, together, agree that there is more to it all than this.

OPTIMAL FUNCTIONING

Although there may be no prescription for healthy living to be found in Kelly's approach to counselling, in his two volumes and in later writing (1967, 1977) he puts forward some very clear ideas as to what might be achieved in terms of the development not only of clients but of those involved with them in the process of reconstruction. When he speaks of 'optimal functioning', as Epting and Amerikaner (1980) point out, Kelly means more than the fulfilling of a person's current potential implied by such notions as self-actualisation. He goes beyond the awakening of dormant attributes and talents to the on-going discovery of new possibilities through active enquiry and experiment, through the person's creation of aspects of the self which never before existed.

In effect, this potential is so great that no one person can achieve it in a single lifetime. We are also constrained by the limitations of our construing system that is involved in all this exploration and experiment. The process is a matter of continually seeing possibilities and making the kinds of choices that both extend the person and remain sufficiently compatible with the self he or she already knows. Few of us will reach out into the unknown without remaining to some extent in contact with something which is known. It follows that this process is not random but has within it a tangible structure, which Kelly calls the 'full cycle of experience'. This is described in Chapter 3 (pp. 45–6), with its phases of *anticipation* of an event, *commitment* or self-involvement, *encounter* with the event, *confirmation* or *disconfirmation* of the expected outcome and, finally, *constructive revision*.

THE EXPERIENCE OF TESSA

An example of such a cycle is the experience of Tessa, who had been deeply troubled by continual failure in relationships. She had been depressed and anxious for some time when she came for counselling, felt herself totally isolated and empty, finding satisfaction neither in her work nor her few friendships. Despite the bleakness of her outlook, though, it was clear that she had made a number of choices in her life which had, among other things, moved her on from a limited background of opportunity to the development of considerable skills in writing and editing. Socially, she felt that she was inept and unattractive and her few relationships with men had 'petered out'. Although not hopeful, her frustration seemed to hold some energy and there was a real wish for something different.

Construing the Possibilities

I (Peggy) began by exploring with her what potential aspects of herself seemed to be undeveloped. She said that she gave nothing to others, no one would really miss her if she were gone. So was this just an understandable need to be needed? No. She saw it as something more important and creative than that; something to do with a reason for being here at all. When I questioned her further this was clearly not an 'ought' imposed from the outside. She had not been brought up with the idea that service to others was a crucial part of existence. It just seemed to her to be a proper part of life.

I asked her in what direction her contribution to others might lie. To begin with, Tessa was blank and then came back with a memory of a programme she had seen on television about music therapy. She had been very moved by the effect of music on some people who were cut off both from their feelings and their potential for growth.

She had not mentioned before that she could play several wind instruments. For a long time she had neglected her playing as there was no one to listen and she did not please herself. How could she know whether she was good enough as a musician and had potential as a music therapist? She could only risk being evaluated by those who trained music therapists. With impressive determination Tessa had some lessons to revive her playing and felt ready to apply for a course.

Anticipating the Outcome of Choice

Before she did so, I asked her to look at the implications of her choice. She thought she would be accepted and when we role played the prospective interview about her reasons for wanting to train she was able to elaborate them with some depth. The outcome was not a forgone conclusion, of course, and there was the risk of her *not* being accepted, but she felt that it was a risk worth taking. So she was anticipating clearly and ready to commit herself to the challenge, which she encountered with much anxiety but a good deal of excitement. She was accepted and although her expectations were confirmed, some reconstruction was necessary when she learned more about what the course entailed.

Before she embarked on it we looked at her anticipations again and her greatest concerns were to do with relationships with her teachers and others on the course. Our work was then focused on how she might manage these differently from earlier relationships. Largely through the use of role play again, it emerged that she lacked skill in construing what others might be thinking. The development of greater sociality became the major aim of counselling at this point.

Encounter With the Experience

There was no doubt about her commitment to the experience when it came and her encounter with it over the first six months brought her some stress and self-questioning. Gradually, however, she became more comfortable not only with the work but with all the people involved. Some of her expectations were confirmed, some disconfirmed and she had a good deal of constructive revision to do.

She grew in assurance as the course went on and loved the work. She learned to relate well not only to those in need of help but to her peers. Then came the moment when she was qualified and about to embark on a new career. The cycle of experience began again . . .

Not everyone is able to complete these cycles and their functioning may, for the time being at least, remain less than optimal. Tom, for example, came with a similar discontent with his lot and a seemingly fervent wish for change. He felt that his life was useless and longed for something more meaningful. In his case, however, although ideas were plentiful and his anticipations of events frequently elaborated, he had the greatest difficulty in commitment – it was safer to dream of possible new horizons than to move towards them.

For a long time Rachel, another client, was willing to experiment with new ideas and even to commit herself to action. But she could not deal with the disconfirmation of her expectations and backed off from her experience in a hostile way, unwilling to revise her construing. Later, however, she was more able not only to make better predictions about the outcomes of choices she made, but to bear invalidation and take steps to reconstrue and start again.

THE COUNSELLOR'S EXPERIENCE

Since we have referred to the importance of reflexivity throughout this book, we cannot leave this question of the full cycle of experience without emphasising that the counsellor too needs to complete these stages in relation to work with any client. Kelly (1977: 12), speaking of his own role as a clinical psychologist, maintains:

Except as I involve myself deeply with the person whose life is at a turning point, unless I seek to anticipate the outcomes of his decisions at this point, unless I myself make some commitment to joining him in a common undertaking, and unless in this situation I am ready to *reconstrue* psychology rather than *apply* it merely, then I think that as a psychologist, I shall accomplish little more than to accumulate a bibliography to attach to my next application for a job.

For 'psychologist' read 'counsellor', for 'psychology' read 'counselling' and for 'bibliography' read 'case history'. We too, like Tom, may fail to commit ourselves fully and, like Rachel, be unwilling to acknowledge the need for reconstruction if we are not deeply enough involved in what we do.

THE ROLE OF COUNSELLING IN OPTIMAL FUNCTIONING

Clearly, how far each person will go in following through these full cycles of experience will depend on a number of factors, the main one perhaps being the capacity to deal with the anxiety and threat involved. We have referred to the importance of maintaining a sense of the known self through these ventures and not everyone is able to risk a great deal of challenge. So how do we know when a person has, for the time being, reached a certain potential beyond which we cannot help them go? The answer is, we do not, and it is certainly not for us as counsellors ever to judge another's ultimate possibilities. But there must come a time when we and our clients bring an end to the work we do together. Some come with a specific problem and are happy to leave when that has been addressed. Others journey further with us and will, we hope, continue the journey and go on alone or in company with others in their lives.

PERSONAL CONSTRUCT COUNSELLING AS A UNIQUE PERIOD OF CHANGE

A period of involvement in counselling will be neither the beginning nor the end of the process of change for any client. However 'stuck' they may be when they come for help they bring with them a lifetime of experience and a system of construing, which has already changed and developed in many ways. We have emphasised throughout this book that the counselling sessions themselves are only a part of the work undertaken during this period by both client and counsellor and that what happens between sessions forms much of the 'action'. And it should be clear that, working in such a partnership, any change has only partly to do with the understanding and involvement of the counsellor. Nevertheless, there are features of this joint enterprise as Kelly conceived it which make such a period of change distinct from any other in a person's life.

The relationship between the two people is such that the focus is on the concerns of the client only, unlike the shared experience of friendship or family relationships. The counsellor's personal view of things is suspended and, in its place, a professional system for subsuming the views of the client is brought to bear. It is these professional constructs which guide the counsellor as to the nature and timing of specific interventions. The personal construct framework also provides the structure of the counselling series and the pace at which movement is attempted. Areas for work are chosen in the light of the degree of anxiety and threat likely to be involved. Awareness of the client's experience of guilt or hostility, and assessment of their capacity for loosening or tightening their construing, lead the counsellor to help the client maintain a fragile status quo at one point and encourage aggression at another.

Although many changes in a person's life may be carefully planned, others occur through a less purposeful response to circumstances, often without a great deal of awareness of what is going on. When people feel immobilised and confused, the clarification and the structure offered through regular meetings and agreed aims may bring a reassuring stability to an otherwise chaotic period of life. At the same time, within that secure framework, there is the opportunity to get in touch with a whole range of feelings without fear of reprisals, space to let go of restricting ways of viewing events, the chance to dare to imagine how things might be. It is this combination of security and freedom together with the nature of the relationship which makes personal construct counselling a context fruitful for psychological change.

SUMMARY

In this chapter we have considered the issues involved in drawing a period of counselling to a close. We have looked at the indicators of a client's readiness to move on and suggested ways in which the changes made may be reviewed and expectations of the future clarified. The role of counselling in optimal functioning has been discussed together with our view of such counselling as offering a unique period of change.

REFERENCES

Bannister, D. (1962) 'The nature and measurement of schizophrenic thought disorder', *Journal of Mental Science*, 108: 825–42.

Bannister, D. (1977) 'The logic of passion', in D. Bannister (ed.), *New Perspectives in Personal Construct Theory*. London: Academic Press.

Bannister, D. and Fransella, F. (1986) *Inquiring Man* (3rd edition). London: Croom Helm.

Butler, R. and Green, D. (1998) *The Child Within*. Oxford: Butterworth-Heinemann.

Dalton, P. and Dunnett, G. (1992) *A Psychology for Living*. Chichester: John Wiley. Reprinted by EPCA Publications, Farnborough, 1999.

Epting, F.R. (1984) *Personal Construct Counselling and Psychotherapy*. Chichester: John Wiley.

Epting, F.R. and Amerikaner, M. (1980) 'Optimal functioning: a personal construct approach', in A.W. Landfield and L. Leitner (eds), *Personal Construct Psychology: Psychotherapy and Personality*. New York: John Wiley.

Fransella, F. (1972) *Personal Change and Reconstruction: Research on a Treatment of Stuttering*. London: Academic Press.

Fransella, F. (1981) 'Nature babbling to herself: the self characterisation as a psychotherapeutic tool', in H. Bonarius, R. Holland and S. Rosenberg (eds), *Personal Construct Psychology: Recent Advances in Theory and Practice*. London: Macmillan.

Fransella, F. (1985) 'Death by starvation', in W. Dryden (ed.), *Therapists' Dilemmas*. London: Sage Publications.

Fransella, F. (1995) *George Kelly*. London: Sage Publications.

Fransella, F. and Adams, B. (1966) 'An illustration of the use of repertory grid technique in a clinical setting', *British Journal of Social and Clinical Psychology*, 5: 51–62

Fransella, F. and Bannister, D. (1977) *A Manual for Repertory Grid Technique*. London: Academic Press.

Hinkle, D. (1965) 'The change of personal constructs from the viewpoint of a theory of construct implications'. Unpublished PhD thesis, Ohio State University.

Jones, H. (1985) 'Creativity and depression: an idiographic study', in F. Epting and A.W. Landfield (eds), *Anticipating Personal Construct Psychology*. Lincoln: University of Nebraska Press.

Kelly, G.A. (1955/1991) *The Psychology of Personal Constructs*. New York: Norton. Reprinted by Routledge, London, 1991.

Kelly, G.A. (1958) 'Personal construct theory and the psychotherapeutic interview', in B. Maher (ed.), *Clinical Psychology and Personality*. Florida: Krieger.

Kelly, G.A. (1967) 'A psychology of optimal man', in B. Maher (ed.), *The Goals of Psychotherapy*. New York: Appleton-Century-Crofts.

Kelly, G.A. (1969a) 'The autobiography of a theory', in B. Maher (ed.), *Clinical Psychology and Personality*. Florida: Krieger.

Kelly, G.A. (1969b) 'Humanistic methodology in psychological research', in B. Maher (ed.), *Clinical Psychology and Personality*. Florida: Krieger.

Kelly, G.A. (1969c) 'The psychotherapeutic relationship', in B. Maher (ed.), *Clinical Psychology and Personality*. Florida: Krieger.

Kelly, G.A. (1969d) 'The language of hypothesis: man's psychological instrument', in B. Maher (ed.) *Clinical Psychology and Personality*. Florida: Krieger.

Kelly, G.A. (1977) 'The psychology of the unknown', in D. Bannister (ed.), *New Perspectives in Personal Construct Theory*. London: Academic Press.

Kelly, G.A. (1986a) *A Brief Introduction to Personal Construct Theory*. London: Centre for Personal Construct Psychology.

Kelly, G.A. (1986b) *Behaviour is an Experiment*. London: Centre for Personal Construct Psychology.

Landfield, A.W. (1971) *Personal Construct Systems in Psychotherapy*. Chicago: Rand McNally.

Leitner, L.M. (1985) 'Interview methodologies for construct elicitation: searching for the core', in F. Epting and A.W. Landfield (eds), *Anticipating Personal Construct Psychology*. Lincoln: University of Nebraska Press.

Maher, B. (1969) *Clinical Psychology and Personality*. Florida: Krieger.

Maher, B. (1985) Personal communication.

Neimeyer, R. (1980) 'George Kelly as therapist: a review of his tapes', in A.W. Landfield and L.M. Leitner (eds), *Personal Construct Psychology: Psychotherapy and Personality*. Toronto: Wiley.

Neimeyer, R.A. (1998) *Lessons of Loss: a Guide to Coping*. New York: McGraw-Hill.

Ravenette, A.T. (1999) 'A drawing and its opposite', in *Personal Construct Theory in Educational Psychology: a Practitioner's View*. London: Whurr Publishers.

Ryle, A. and Lunghi, M.E. (1970) 'The dyad grid: a modification of repertory grid technique', *British Journal of Psychiatry*, 177: 323–7.

Thorman, C. (1983) *Constructs*, Vol. 2, no. 1. Newsletter of the Centre for Personal Construct Psychology.

Tschudi, F. (1977) 'Loaded and honest questions: a construct theory view of symptoms and therapy', in D. Bannister (ed.), *New Perspectives in Personal Construct Theory*. London: Academic Press.

Tschudi, F. and Sandsberg, S. (1984) 'On the advantages of symptoms: exploring the client's construing', *Scandinavian Journal of Psychology*, 25: 169–77.

Viney, L. (1989) *Images of Illness* (2nd edition). Florida: Krieger.

Zelhart, P. and Thomas, T.T. (1983) 'George A. Kelly, 1931–1943: environmental influences on a developing theorist', in J. Adams-Webber and J.C. Mancuso (eds), *Applications of Personal Construct Theory*. Ontario: Academic Press.

Index